PLANNING THE FINANCES OF THE HEALTH SECTOR

A manual for developing countries

by

E. P. Mach
*Division of Strengthening
of Health Services
World Health Organization
Geneva, Switzerland*

B. Abel-Smith
*London School of Economics
and Political Science
London, England*

WORLD HEALTH ORGANIZATION
GENEVA
1983

PRINTED IN SWITZERLAND

83/5672 – Imprimeries Réunies S.A. Lausanne – 6000

CONTENTS

	Page
Preface	5
Acknowledgements	7
Chapter 1. Introduction	9
The development of health policies	9
Health for all by the year 2000	10
The analysis of national health expenditure and sources of finance	12
Chapter 2. Definitions	15
Personal health services	15
Health-related activities	17
Capital and recurrent expenditure	17
Sources of finance	18
Categories of health expenditure	19
Chapter 3. Study objectives	21
Policy relevance	21
Some uses of data	24
Conclusion	29
Chapter 4. Planning a study	31
Initial preparations	31
Timetable and schedule of work	33
Record keeping	33
Specification of terms of reference	34
Specification of research objectives and data organization	34
Chapter 5. Data collection	39
Ministry of health	39
Other ministries and local government	43

Compulsory health insurance (social security) 48
Voluntary health insurance 50
Missions 51
Employers 51
Local voluntary bodies 52
Direct private payments 53
Self-help and other private sources 57
External cooperation 57
Financial flows 60
Small surveys and samples 63

Chapter 6. Primary health care 71
Definition 71
Data collection 73
Classification by source of finance 76

Chapter 7. Evaluation and the examination of alternatives . . 79
Evaluation of the material collected 79
Planning for the extra resources required for the growth of
    priority programmes 83
Conclusion 93

Chapter 8. Projections of future expenditure and sources
    of finance 95
Primary health care 97
Secondary and tertiary services 98
The presentation of options 99
Conclusion 101

References and further reading 105

Annex 1. Examples of completed tables 107
Recurrent expenditures 107
Expenditure on primary health care 109
Capital expenditures 109
Broad aspects of data analysis and interpretation 110

Annex 2. Analysis of completed tables 115
Purpose of expenditure 115

PREFACE

Many countries, particularly in the developing world, are seeking to orientate their health services towards a more equitable and efficient utilization of resources. A detailed analysis of the financing of health services is an important step in such an undertaking.

This manual sets out a methodology for carrying out such an analysis, suggesting ways of collecting and organizing data on expenditure and sources of finance. It also suggests how this information might be utilized in policy formulation—to make a master plan for the future use of all financial and material resources. Particular attention is paid to primary health care in view of its high priority in current health policies. A series of tables presents models that provide an analytical framework for national planning, and summary tables have been devised for the use of policymakers.

The manual is aimed at planners, economists, statisticians, accountants and researchers in the health and health-related sectors in developing countries, and at the staff of international and bilateral agencies concerned with development aid. It is hoped that the results of periodic studies undertaken with the help of this manual will assist policy-makers in taking decisions. It is also hoped that the methodology, or part of it, will serve for routine data collection and presentation and thus enable trends to be analysed over longer periods of time. Furthermore, the manual is intended to serve as training material for the different categories of personnel mentioned above, as part of the general policy of strengthening national capacities in all areas, including planning, management and the evaluation of the health system. National and international organizers of workshops, seminars and training courses in these fields, both in the health sector and beyond in general planning and national financial management, may find this manual, or an adapted version of it, of use in their work.

Many national case studies and a number of international workshops have contributed to the evolution of this manual. The basic assumption was made that, even with limited statistical data, useful estimates could be made of the main categories of health expenditure, sources of finance, and the flows of money within the health sector, and that this information could help policy-makers and managers to take appropriate action. It was suggested that data on expenditure and sources of finance should be collected by reviewing the finances of the most visible providers of health care, e.g., ministries of health, other ministries, local authorities, social security schemes, religious missions and private practitioners. This approach has been adopted and further developed. In particular, methods have been added for estimating the value of transactions in the private health sector, assessing the level and sources of foreign assistance, estimating the expenditure on safe drinking-water supply, sanitation and nutrition programmes, and classifying costs and finances of primary health care and analysing the findings.

The chapters on financial forecasts and on possible ways of taking corrective action give brief descriptions of options currently being chosen in some countries, and do not provide a complete list of possible solutions. In particular, Chapter 8 gives only an outline of projections of future expenditure and sources of finance. It is hoped that greater detail will emerge with descriptions of further national experiences.

This manual has been widely circulated for comments and the subject was discussed at a number of international workshops—among others, in Mexico (interregional, 1979), India (for countries of the South-East Asia Region, 1979), Colombia (for countries of the Americas, 1979) and the Philippines (for countries of the Western Pacific Region, 1982). Teaching material was also developed for an intercountry training course in Botswana on techniques of surveying health finance.

ACKNOWLEDGEMENTS

The contributions of the following persons and institutions are greatly appreciated: representatives of the governments of the countries where national case studies were undertaken, in particular Dr R. Alvarez Gutiérrez, Dr R. A. Gomaa, and Dr D. Sebina, who sponsored country case studies and workshops on health services financing, and Mr M. Mills, responsible for the second case study in Botswana; members of the study group and advisory group, in particular Mr M. Kam, who served as the focal point for the first case study in Botswana, described its methodology and prepared the first draft of this manual; Professor O. de la Grandville, Professor A. Laurent, Professor M. Roemer and Mr van Amstel; participants in an inter-regional workshop on financing of health services (Mexico, 1979), a regional consultation of the research programme on financing of health care delivery in South-East Asia (1979), and a seminar on financing health care development (Manila, 1982); the Sandoz Institute for Health and Socio-Economic Studies, for its financial and technical support to national case studies; participants in an intercountry workshop in Botswana; the American Public Health Association for supporting conferences and studies on the subject; the Office of International Health, United States Department of Health and Human Services; Mr J. Warford, Ms A. Mashayekhi and Mr D. De Ferranti for testing the manual at country assignments for the World Bank and making comments; experts who contributed through their studies, papers and publications; the WHO staff at headquarters and regional offices and the WHO project coordinators.

CHAPTER 1

Introduction

The development of health policies

In the early 1950s many developing countries were concentrating their efforts on the eradication of diseases through mass campaigns run outside the main structure of their health services. As early as 1953, WHO was stressing the need to strengthen basic health services "to meet the most urgent problems affecting large sections of the population" (23). During the 1960s a number of developing countries integrated their special programmes with their basic health services.

Progress in developing basic health services—particularly in rural health services—has been slow and uneven. A joint UNICEF/WHO study reported in 1975 that, despite great efforts, the basic needs of vast numbers of people throughout the world were still unmet (7). Too often the pattern of health services has been modelled on those in industrialized countries—relatively sophisticated services staffed by highly qualified personnel. These services have been concentrated in the cities and towns, have been predominantly curative, and have catered for only a small minority of the population. It has not proved possible to expand effective access to services of this type to anything like the entire population.

Several World Health Assemblies have stressed that an alternative approach can be practicable and relatively successful if:

(1) The emphasis is switched from urban to rural populations and to the underprivileged.

(2) Services are integrated, combining both curative and preventive strategies as part of wider socioeconomic development.

(3) The importance for health of sanitation, housing, nutrition, education and communication is given full recognition.

(4) The use of services is promoted where local populations take a

major responsibility for them both in providing manpower and facilities and in participating in decisions on local health policies.

(5) Locally recruited primary health care workers, supported by their communities, can form the front line of the health care system.

(6) The work of indigenous healers is given full recognition.

Health for all by the year 2000

In 1977, the World Health Assembly decided that the main social target of governments and WHO should be "the attainment by all the citizens of the world by the year 2000 of a level of health that will permit them to lead a socially and economically productive life" (resolution WHA30.43). In 1978, a conference held in Alma-Ata, USSR, declared that primary health care was the key to attaining this target (27).

The conference defined primary health care as essential health care made universally accessible to individuals and families by means acceptable to them, through their full participation, and at a cost that the community and country could afford.

These services were to include as a minimum:

(1) education concerning health problems and methods to prevent and control them;

(2) promotion of food supply and proper nutrition;

(3) an adequate supply of safe water, and basic sanitation;

(4) maternal and child health care, including family planning;

(5) immunization against the major infectious diseases;

(6) prevention and control of locally endemic diseases;

(7) appropriate treatment of common diseases and injuries;

(8) provision of essential drugs.

In 1979, the World Health Assembly invited the Member States of WHO to formulate national, regional and global strategies, a health strategy having been described by the WHO Executive Board as "the broad lines of action required in all sectors to give effect to health policy". The Global Strategy published in 1981 (22) started from country strategies and was built up through regions to the world level. It is a synthesis of ideas derived from national and regional strategies.[1] The main thrusts of the Strategy are:

— primary health care to deliver programmes that reach the *whole* population;

---

[1] The Global Strategy is referred to throughout as "the Strategy".

— action to be taken by individuals, families and communities as well as by health services and health-related services in other sectors;

— technology that is appropriate, scientifically sound, adaptable, acceptable to users, and within the capacity of the country to afford;

— a high degree of community involvement;

— international action to support national action.

Action is also specified to promote and support the Strategy:

— by disseminating information to maintain population support;

— by ensuring political commitment at every level;

— by enlisting the support of the relevant professionals;

— by strengthening the health arm of government;

— by developing the managerial process;

— by reorienting the national research effort;

— by mobilizing human resources;

— by generating the necessary finance, including transfers from developed to developing countries;

— by creating the necessary international cooperation.

A list of indicators has been prepared to monitor progress in implementing the Strategy at every level (20).

WHO will provide coordination and promote technical cooperation and the Organization will be restructured accordingly. Its programmes of work will give high priority to the support of the Strategy. WHO will use the Strategy to support the International Development Strategy for the Third Development Decade, thus contributing to the New International Economic Order.

For this manual, the following sections of the Strategy (22; pp. 67–68) are particularly relevant:

"Just as the successful implementation of the Strategy will mean mobilizing all possible human resources, it will also depend on mobilizing all possible financial and material resources. This implies first of all making the most efficient use of existing resources both within and among countries. At the same time, additional resources will undoubtedly have to be generated.

In this context *ministries of health* will:

(1) review the distribution of their health budget and in particular allocations to primary health care and intermediate and central levels, to urban and rural areas, and to specific underserved groups;

(2) reallocate existing resources as necessary—or, if this proves impossible, at least allocate any additional resources—for the provision of primary health care, particularly for underserved population groups;

(3) include an analysis of needs in terms of costs and material in all consideration of health technology and of the establishment and maintenance of the health infrastructure;

11

(4) consider the benefit of various health programmes in relation to the cost, as well as the effectiveness of different technologies and different ways of organizing the health system in relation to the cost;

(5) estimate the order of magnitude of the total financial needs to implement the national strategy up to the year 2000;

(6) attempt to secure additional national funds for the strategy if necessary and if they are convinced that they can prove that they have made the best possible use of existing funds;

(7) consider alternative ways of financing the health system, including the possible use of social security funds;

(8) identify activities that might attract external grants or loans;

(9) in developing countries take action so that their governments request such grants and loans from external banks, funds and multilateral and bilateral agencies;

(10) in developed countries, take action to influence the agencies concerned to provide such grants and loans;

(11) *present to their government a master plan for the use of all financial and material resources, including government direct and indirect financing; social security and health insurance schemes; local community solutions in terms of energy, labour, materials and cash; individual payments for service; and the use of external loans and grants.*" [1]

The analysis of national health expenditure and sources of finance

How should a master plan be prepared for the use of all financial and material resources? The first step is to obtain a clear picture of the use of current financial and material resources, identifying allocations to primary health care, to intermediate and central levels, to urban and rural areas and to specific underserved groups. The full costs of various health programmes are not always known, as support costs (such as transport, the maintenance of buildings, and supervision) may fall on other budgets or other parts of the budget. A master plan of all financial and material resources will normally involve data stretching far outside the ministry of health budget into the budgets of other government departments, compulsory health insurance agencies, industry, voluntary bodies and the private sector. Extremely few developing countries, and by no means all developed countries, know all that is spent on health services and health-related activities and how these services are being financed.

The budgets of ministries of health, in their conventional structure, are not suitable for policy analysis since they normally consist only of

---

[1] Authors' italics.

a breakdown into such categories as personnel, supplies and equipment, transportation and training. In addition, they often reflect an intention to spend rather than authority to spend. The amount actually spent is ascertainable only after the year is over. How it was spent can only be ascertained by examining a wide range of other information.

While, in principle, the ministry is responsible for the health of all citizens of the country, usually it has direct authority only over its own services and programmes and the funds allotted to it. It has no right to decide on the use of funds by other ministries or public agencies, though they may fund important health-related activities such as nutrition, water supply and sanitation programmes. Even more limited is the ministry of health's ability to influence the way funds are used in the private sector. Nevertheless, in many countries the ministry of health is responsible for the preparation and implementation of national health development plans for the whole health sector, including the allocation of resources; this is one of the reasons why the ministry of health needs to know about all expenditure in the sector and all sources of finance.

In most developing countries information about the private sector is scarce or incomplete. Yet attitudes to its role are seldom neutral; most countries have at least implicit policies towards it. In some countries it is regarded as an asset: private providers lighten the load on the public sector by looking after those who can afford to pay. In others, it is regarded as a liability—robbing the public sector of skilled manpower, usually trained at public expense, and thus increasing the gap in the health provisions between the rich and the poor. Planning for the entire health sector is possible only if expenditure in all sectors is brought together.

In many countries the different financial sectors of the national health effort operate in watertight compartments even when there are monetary flows between them. Each sector goes its own way with little coordination let alone joint planning between them. This can be true of ministries of health, compulsory health insurance agencies, private insurers, voluntary bodies, industrial and agricultural employers which provide health services and, particularly, external donors of funds. Coordination can be strengthened by bringing all those concerned into the planning process. One way of showing the role of each sector is in the form of a master budget which can in turn be used to build a master plan for future expenditures.

Hence it is suggested that countries need to undertake periodic studies of expenditure and sources of finance in their health sector as an integral part of the national planning process. The aim should be to identify broad orders of magnitude rather than to attempt precise accounting to each unit of national currency. This inevitably involves a considerable amount of estimating such as underlies other widely used figures, for example, those of national income or national product. Thus low-cost and relatively swift studies are envisaged rather than protracted and meticulous surveys.

Such studies can, depending on the extent to which the data are developed, form the basis of a master plan by:

— identifying where health policy objectives are being promoted or frustrated by the nature, size or appropriateness of different sources of finance;

— showing where resources could be used more efficiently;

— demonstrating any lack of equity in the use of resources in both the public and the private sector;

— drawing attention to where alternative ways of finding further resources need to be found;

— quantifying the gap between the financial resources likely to be obtained, given existing policies, and the resources needed to move decisively towards specific long-term goals during the medium-term period.

CHAPTER 2

Definitions

In this chapter, definitions are given of personal health services and health-related activities and of capital and recurrent expenditure. Sources of finances are explained and the main categories of health expenditure are defined.

It is useful to make a distinction between *personal health services* (services to improve the health of identifiable persons) and *health-related activities* (which promote the health of the population collectively). This is not because one category is necessarily more important than the other but because the activities are of a different character. The distinction is not always clear-cut. Moreover, in view of the wide range of activities that have some influence on health, any attempt to draw a line around health-related activities must inevitably be a matter of somewhat arbitrary convention. This chapter suggests general criteria but does not attempt to cover every possible provision that may be encountered in every country. Inevitably, decisions will have to be made at the national level on particular arrangements in each country. What is important is that all decisions should be carefully recorded so that those undertaking later studies in the same country can produce data comparable with those for earlier years.

Personal health services

Obviously these include the services to persons provided by health-trained personnel, the cost of the buildings and supplies they use and the other personnel who work with them. The services may be preventive, curative or rehabilitative. The cost of training the personnel is part of the cost of providing the services. But what about traditional practitioners who are apprenticed rather than trained, and herbal remedies where evidence of effectiveness is not available? It is proposed that services should be defined in terms of *purpose* rather than *achievement*. Even 'the most highly skilled care may not improve the health of a particular individual. Thus all services purchased or used for the purpose of health improvement should be classified as personal health services.

This does not dispose of all the problems. Fine distinctions should in theory be made in the following cases, although they may not apply exactly if the available data are not classified in this way:

(1) *Health improvement and personal care:* the distinction between services to improve health and the ordinary maintenance of the body. Sunglasses may be used for medical or cosmetic purposes. Vitamins may be prescribed or taken as a regular food supplement.

(2) *What is a hospital?* A hospital is an institution under medical and/or nursing supervision. Cases requiring hospitalization may be cared for in social welfare institutions which provide some nursing and a visiting doctor but are not considered part of the health services.

(3) *Social work:* a fine distinction may need to be made between medical social work and other social work not counted as a health service.

(4) *Education of the public:* a line will need to be drawn between health education and general education even though the latter may include some teaching on health.

(5) *Education of personnel:* a borderline is needed between specialist education and training of health personnel and basic or more general scientific education.

In addition to the normally recognized personal health services, the following are customarily included:

(1) specialist education, training and upgrading of all health personnel;

(2) health research, including biomedical and epidemiological research, and research on the functioning of personal health services;

(3) health education of the public (e.g., personal and home hygiene, transmission of communicable diseases, first aid, nutrition);

(4) rehabilitation, orthopaedic and prosthetic devices and appliances for the handicapped;

(5) family planning services;

(6) expenditure on health practitioners, including traditional practitioners and midwives, and on self-treatment (whether with herbs, patent medicines or traditional remedies); and, where possible, volun-

tary labour and materials given to promote or support personal health services.

Health-related activities

It would not be useful to include all expenditures which might contribute to health, for example, all expenditure on food, housing and water supplies. Many people spend much more on housing and food than is necessary for health and some water supplies are used for agricultural purposes. The aim should be to include expenditures on nutrition, water supplies and sanitation which: (*a*) have a clear health purpose; and (*b*) are primarily to meet basic needs.

The following are customarily included, although this list is not exhaustive:

(1) expenditure on the construction of rural and peri-urban water and sanitation facilities designed to meet basic health needs;

(2) expenditure on health inspection and public sanitation and other measures for the prevention of communicable diseases (e.g., refuse collection and disposal, port health control);

(3) expenditure to control zoonotic (animal) diseases for the protection of human beings;

(4) expenditure to promote safety at work and combat occupational disease;

(5) expenditure on nutritional supplements to individuals at risk;

(6) expenditure on food subsidies to help secure that basic needs are met;

(7) expenditure to secure the provision of basic housing at prices that can be afforded.

Capital and recurrent expenditure

In both personal health services and health-related activities a distinction should be made between capital and recurrent expenditure. Expenditure on water supply or on basic housing can be capital or recurrent. In general, the acquisition of a durable asset with a life of more than one year, such as land, buildings, equipment, vehicles and furniture, is counted as capital expenditure. Some countries include within recurrent expenditure the depreciation and interest charges on capital assets—the annual cost of the use of the assets. This item should be separately identified. It is not appropriate to add together some items of expenditure that include depreciation and interest charges and some that do not. In national totals, depreciation and interest should be either included in all cases or completely excluded.

Sources of finance

It is not suggested that attempts should be made in studies of this kind to trace back funds to their original sources (e.g., to determine which income groups pay the taxes or health insurance contributions that finance personal health services and health-related activities) unless this is a specific research objective. It is rather proposed that funds should be classified according to the agency that originally provided them. Thus grants from central government to compulsory or voluntary health insurance or to local government, or from central or local government to voluntary bodies, are classified as the funds of the grant provider rather than the spender. Funds coming from abroad should be separately identified, though they may be channelled through government or voluntary bodies (e.g., mission hospitals or agencies providing family planning).

In whatever way resources of finance are classified there is a danger that funds transferred from one source to another may be counted twice. To make sure that such double counting is avoided, provision is made in the model worksheets for transfers to be shown separately. This makes it possible to check how much of the grant was actually received and spent and to calculate on what it was spent. Unless it was earmarked for a specific purpose, it can be regarded as having been spent proportionately on all the services provided by the spending agency. It is the sum spent during the year studied that matters and the classified use of funds can be attributed back to the original source of the funds (e.g., the ministry of health or external aid) in the main summary tables.

Finally, it should be noted that not all resources are provided in the form of money. Some are provided in kind-donated labour and materials. These should be brought into account as far as possible.

18

In most countries all sources of finance can be classified under the following headings:

(a) *Public sources*
  — ministry of health
  — other government departments
  — regional and local government
  — compulsory health insurance

(b) *Private sources*
  — private health insurance
  — private employers
  — local donations (cash)
  — private households
  — donated labour

(c) *External cooperation*
  — official
  — non-official.

Categories of health expenditure

It is normally useful to distinguish five subsectors:

— institutional personal health care (where the patient is resident);

— ambulatory personal health care (services given to non-residents, even in their own homes);

— specialist health programmes (aimed at particular diseases or health problems);

— health-related activities;

— training, management, research and other services.

For each of these categories, use of transport services and the cost of maintaining the necessary buildings should be included.

Over and above this classification, countries will find it useful to have a category "Primary health care" covering the services listed on pages 10 and 11 as a minimum (see also Chapter 6).

CHAPTER 3

Study objectives

Policy relevance

The precise way in which data are broken down in a study of health financing in a particular country should be decided according to the policy objectives of that country. Often there will be more than one objective. For example, priority may be being given to a particular disease, e.g., malaria, or to a particular method of combating a group of diseases, e.g., water and sanitation. At the same time, priority may be being given to improving access to services, by making them more evenly distributed or by reducing or removing price barriers, or to improving efficiency, providing more services out of a given budget.

Policy objectives are expressed in national health plans. The team assigned to make the study should extract from these plans elements capable of being measured in financial terms. For example, the health plan of a developing country in the Western Pacific Region of WHO includes the following:

(a) *Priority health problems*
— nutrition
— water and sanitation
— communicable diseases
— infant mortality

(b) *Distributional priorities*
— greater equity: priority to the rural areas.

Thus a financing study for this country would include an analysis in three dimensions and seek to establish what is being spent on:
— nutrition, water, sanitation, communicable diseases;
— children in the first year of life;
— different geographical areas (divided into urban and rural).

21

This is the basis for planning the future allocation of resources. A later study can evaluate the extent to which expenditures have in fact moved in the planned directions.

Recent plans for an African country stressed:

(a) *Priority health problems*
  — nutrition
  — tuberculosis
  — malaria
  — schistosomiasis
  — sleeping sickness
  — blindness

(b) *Priority services*
  — health education
  — maternal and child health
  — family planning
  — environmental sanitation
  — dental health
  — mental health
  — occupational health
  — services for the handicapped

(c) *Pattern of service priorities*
  — primary health care: capital investment to be directed to building units where none exist rather than upgrading existing units

(d) *Distributional priorities*
  — equity

(e) *Training priorities*
  — staff to improve rural services.

A study for this country should first of all attempt to ascertain what is currently being spent by each source of finance on each of the priority health problems and on each of the priority services. This is the basis for a plan showing how much more is to be spent on these priorities in future years and how this extra expenditure is going to be financed. A later study can evaluate the extent to which additional resources have in fact gone to each of these priorities.

Secondly, a specific calculation of what is being spent on primary health care and a geographical analysis of the pattern of expenditure are required. These again are needed to plan how much more is to be spent each year on primary health care and how to secure greater equity.

Can additional money be found to finance these developments from a variety of possible sources of finance? If not, the plan may need to specify at what rate expenditure on overprovided areas would need to be cut to find resources for underprovided areas, and at what rate other services need to be cut to find resources for the extension of primary health care. One way of making the switch would be by changing methods of financing (e.g., introducing selective charges for secondary care and securing community as well as public contributions to primary health care).

Thirdly, the analysis of capital expenditure needs to separate the building of wholly new primary health care units within the total, so as to form the basis for a plan to expand new building in rural areas. A later survey will be able to establish how much progress has actually been made towards meeting these objectives.

Finally, the study should seek to identify within expenditure on education and training how much is being devoted to staff for rural services. A later survey could examine how far these newly trained staff really were working in rural areas.

Thus the objectives of a health finance study are: to obtain data on expenditure and sources of financing related to the above objectives and on the basis of analysis to recommend action, i.e., redistribution of funds, ways of raising new funds, areas for cost containment, new financing mechanisms, etc. (*19*).

The above example from an African country requires an analysis in five dimensions. This is inevitably complex, but the complexity comes from the plan itself. In a country where no financing study has previously been undertaken, it is advisable not to attempt everything that would be desirable but to select primary topics of interest, according to their importance, balanced against the time and effort required to obtain reasonably reliable data. Thus, in the above example, the analysis by health problem may be too difficult to attempt in a first study; it may need to be omitted with the intention of including it in later surveys, when the statistical system has been developed to produce appropriate data for financial analysis.

Of particular importance in most developing countries is the geographical distribution of health resources. One way of analysing such data is in the form of a table showing the distribution of population by region, province, district, etc., and the ratio of different categories of health manpower per 1000 population and of the health expenditure per head of population. Alternatively, these data can be superimposed on a map which might also include epidemiological data of special importance in the particular country.

In some countries there may be no specific national health plan. However, priorities may have been laid down in speeches of the minister of health in parliament or elsewhere or in statements of policy prepared for prospective donors of foreign aid. Where no written policy statements are available, a statement of health priorities should be requested. A financing study that identifies expenditures on items which are not of any special policy interest is of no value for planning purposes.

Some uses of data

It is not possible to list all the possible analyses that could be undertaken for particular policy purposes, nor is it suggested that any one study should attempt all or nearly all of the types of analysis listed below. The aim of giving these illustrations is to assist countries in choosing which types of analysis would be most useful to them in developing their health plans.

Total health sector expenditure, as a percentage of the gross national product (GNP), gross domestic product (GDP) or net national income (NI), is often used to compare relative spending on different sectors (e.g., health and education) and to measure the growth or decrease in the share of national resources devoted to each sector over time; in some industrialized countries the percentage of GNP between years or relative changes in the pay of health personnel compared with the pay of personnel outside the health sector may considerably change the percentage, without there being any real change in the volume of the country's health effort. Moreover, international comparisons can be misleading because of the difficulties mentioned above of defining health expenditure on a comparable basis. The Global Strategy for health for all by the year 2000 will be using as an indicator the number of countries spending 5% or more of GNP on health.

Total public sector expenditure on personal health services as a percentage of GNP

This can be used for rough international comparisons, bearing in mind that most data so far published only cover expenditures by the ministry of health.

In a review of health expenditure in November 1981, the Director-General of the World Health Organization [1] quoted the following figures:

"For public spending only, 19 out of the 25 least developed countries spend less than 1.5% of GNP on health, while none of them spends more than 2.8% of their GNP on health; 48 out of the other 85 developing countries spend less than 1.5% and 2 out of 85 more than 4% of their GNP on health."

Total public sector expenditure on health (PSEH) as a proportion of total public expenditure

This contains the expenditures of the ministry of health, other government agencies and compulsory health insurance (including funds from external cooperation channelled through government). One use of this indicator is to compare the health sector's share of public expenditure with that of other sectors (education, agriculture, defence, etc.). The trend (increase, decrease or unchanged) can provide an indication of the past policy of government in allocating funds. Unless there has been a change in policy, this may indicate the level of funding that can be expected from government in the future.

Total PSEH versus total private sector expenditure on health

This comparison has a number of possible uses. Firstly, it shows what people are prepared to spend privately on health compared with what is compulsorily collected and allocated for health. A substantial part of this expenditure may go on traditional services. The improvement of these services and their coordination with the organized services might secure a considerable improvement in health. Substantial expenditure may be going on imported drugs. Restricting what is available in the private drug market on the basis of cost-effectiveness is one way of reducing imports. Some private spending might be

---
[1] *Review of health expenditures.* Report by the Director-General to the Executive Board, 1981 (unpublished WHO document EB69/7).

"captured" by the organized sector by charging for certain services (with systems of exemption from the charges, e.g., for "the poor"). A further policy option, not acceptable in some countries, is to find ways of encouraging more of the better-off to use private services (e.g., by the development of private health insurance) so that more of the publicly financed services are available to be used by those with modest financial resources. The relative trends over time in the two sectors can be examined to see whether they correspond to policy objectives. Plans can be made for the relative development of the two sectors in the future (see Chapter 7).

Percentage of PSEH devoted to tertiary, secondary and primary health care

This can be used to form the basis of plans for the relative role of the three sectors in the future. Past trends can be examined to see whether they have been in accordance with policy objectives.

A further analysis can be made of institutional care, by different types of facility, and the relevant costs of similar units compared to assess efficiency (e.g., in terms of cost per bed day).

Percentage of PSEH devoted to particular age and sex groups (to the extent that expenditure can be divided in this way)

The age groups might be 0–1 year, 2–5, 6–10, 11–15, 16–25, 26–45, 46–65 and over 66 years. This would make it possible to see the extent to which a priority (e.g., for young children) is in fact being observed and form the basis of plans for greater priority to this particular age group. The data can also be used to calculate the changes in expenditure needed to provide the same level of services to different age and sex groups, as the demographic structure of the population changes over future years, using projections of the population.

Percentage of PSEH devoted to particular regions or districts

This is to assess how equitably resources are distributed in geographical terms and between urban and rural areas. If information is available (e.g., on a sample basis), the allocation should be based on the use of services made by the population of different regions or districts. It cannot be assumed that a unit sited in a particular region or district is exclusively used by the population resident in that region or district and not by that of adjoining regions or districts. Corrections need to be made for cross-boundary movements of users to obtain services. The results can be expressed in terms of expenditure per head of population in particular geographical areas and compared with a planned distribution based on health needs.

Percentage of PSEH devoted to particular income groups

This is to assess equity between various economic groups of the population where data are available from sample surveys. The results can be expressed in terms of expenditure per head in each income group and compared with a planned distribution calculated on the basis of health needs.

Percentage of PSEH devoted to particular selected programmes

Such programmes might, for example be classified,

(a) *by objective:*
— communicable disease control, identifying particular diseases (e.g., malaria)
— mental health
— occupational health
— family planning
— material and child health
— disability and rehabilitation; or

(b) *by type of activity:*
— health education
— immunization
— nutrition
— water
— sanitation
— research (including health services research)
— education and training of personnel, broken down by category. (This analysis can be taken further to calculate the total cost per person of a particular completed training programme, e.g., from short courses for village health workers to long courses for physicians.)

27

Percentage of PSEH devoted to particular types of resources

The categories might include:

(*a*) *Recurrent expenditure on manpower,* broken down by category. From this can be calculated the annual unit cost per doctor, nurse, village health worker, etc. This information is extremely valuable for calculating staffing options. For example, depending on the relative costs, some options for staffing primary health care out of a given budget per 100 000 population might be:

(1) 10 physicians;

(2) 5 physicians, 25 nurses;

(3) 2 physicians, 10 nurses, 100 village health workers.

More elaborate options can be developed using larger numbers of grades of staff.

(*b*) *Equipment,* broken down by category of health facility.

(*c*) *Drugs,* broken down by therapeutic class. (The issue of drugs, their internal production or importation, logistics of distribution, quality control, *per caput* drug expenditure in different regions of a country, and cost of drugs per patient in institutional versus ambulatory care are extremely important for policy analysis, and information available from special studies should be used.)

(*d*) *Transport,* including maintenance costs, petrol, etc. From this it may be possible to calculate the cost per vehicle mile of running different types of vehicle.

(*e*) *Food provided in hospital,* broken down by types of hospital. From this it may be possible to calculate and compare the ingredient cost of food per patient per day in different types of hospital.

Capital expenditure by type of building being constructed and by geographical area

Capital expenditure is particularly important for health planning as any facility (tertiary or district hospital or health centre) will involve recurrent costs once it has been completed and is in use. These costs need to be calculated before the decision is taken to build. This is not always done at present. It has been found that the annual recurrent costs of a hospital amount to a third or more of the capital cost of its construction. The recurrent costs of using new buildings should be fed into plans for recurrent expenditure in later years (see Chapter 7).

Conclusion

Once the sources and levels of finance have been identified and classified, it is possible to consider options for redeploying resources to improve the health of the nation. For example, where compulsory health insurance plays a major role, it may be valuable to undertake a separate analysis of this sector on similar lines to that outlined above for total public sector expenditure on health. Thus, when parallel sets of services are being provided to different sections of the population, comparisons can be made between the distribution and costs of compulsory insurance financed services with those of government financed services. For example, the cost of extending the compulsory health insurance pattern of services to the whole population could be calculated. In some countries, one of the major causes of lack of equity and of maldistribution is the high cost of services provided to those covered by compulsory health insurance compared with the low level of finance provided by government to take care of those who are not covered. This is further discussed in Chapter 7.

In other countries, the relationship between the private sector and the public sector may be a major problem. Key resources of manpower cannot be recruited to work in the public sector, particularly in rural areas, because of the financial and other advantages of working in the private sector. Financing studies can be used to quantify the extent of the problem and policies developed to influence the role of the private sector (see Chapter 7).

In some countries, funds from external cooperation can have effects that distort national priorities. Again, financing studies can be used to identify the extent of the problem. For example, the gift of a hospital will involve recurrent costs that may draw away funds which could alternatively have been used to develop primary health care in rural areas. Projections of cost will show whether it is likely to be possible to find the resources to finance both types of development. If not, policies can be developed accordingly.

In general, financing studies describe how resources are currently being used. It is possible to calculate the gap between the cost of current services and the cost of services planned for the future at different levels of technology. Thus the collection of this information is a first step in planning a projected future distribution of resources and in examining how additional resources might be generated or transferred to pay for this desired pattern of services or how cuts might be made in other sectors to release resources.

CHAPTER 4

Planning a study

Initial preparations

The main steps for making a survey of health expenditure and financing are shown in Fig. 1. The cost of the survey, mainly in staff time, will depend on the amount of detailed information it is decided

Fig. 1. The main steps in making a survey of health expenditure and financing

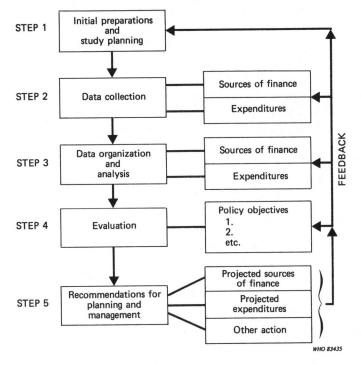

WHO 83435

should be collected. In preparing for a survey, a number of administrative arrangements need to be made.

Personnel

The first decision is which organization and, within that organization, which unit or individuals will be responsible for the survey. The choice will normally depend on the availability of manpower with the requisite skills and experience. Often the ministry of health will be the responsible and coordinating agency. Someone with experience in health economics or health planning may be assigned to take overall responsibility for the study, though the skills of public health administrators, statisticians and accountants may be needed at particular stages. In some countries, it may be advantageous for a national research institute to undertake the survey, with the support of a group of persons who can provide link with other ministries, statistical and planning bureaux, health organizations and other research institutions. Knowledge is required of national development plans and health development plans, of the organization of health services at every level, and of specific accounting and financial procedures. Where necessary, the team may bring in an external expert to give advice on particular aspects of the survey. Moreover, a small number of senior health staff may be needed to act as advisers to the survey team. In some countries, it may be advisable to create two separate teams: one to assemble the data and undertake a preliminary analysis (junior team), and one for final analysis and recommendations (senior team). This arrangement may help to ensure that recommendations are closely related to policy and politically realistic.

As financing studies are of special value when they are periodically repeated, it is highly desirable for there to be a nucleus of staff who will work on later studies.

Logistic support

While the study team is being selected, the coordinating agency should ensure that the necessary support services, secretarial accommodation and supplies, and, where necessary, facilities for travel and subsistence are available to the team. Those from whom information will be sought will need to be informed of the survey so that access is provided to relevant information, and all past and ongoing research that might assist in the study is identified.

Timetable and schedule of work

The team leader should prepare a timetable for the team's activities, indicating the main tasks to be performed, when and by whom. A decision will be required on whether the survey team should make a short-term intensive research effort to the exclusion of their regular duties, or whether the study should be undertaken in conjunction with regular duties over a longer period of time. The team will need to be constituted a number of months before the study report is required. The time period will, however, vary according to the national situation, i.e., a study in a large country with multiple sources of finance and multiple objectives will obviously take longer than one in a small country, or in only a part of a country, or a study with limited research objectives. Once the study has been selected and the precise objectives specified, particular tasks should be assigned to individual team members according to their skills and experience and familiarity with the research topic or area. Regular meetings of team members and/or with supporting groups should be called to review progress and resolve problems. Towards the end of the research period, the team leader, and possibly one or two members of the team, should concentrate exclusively on the organization and analysis of the material, the writing of the report and the drafting of recommendations. This should not take more than one month.

Record keeping

Comprehensive records of the work of the study team should be kept so that later studies can build upon this earlier work. This can be done by:

(*a*) requiring researchers to submit regular and detailed reports to the supporting group;

(*b*) keeping master copies of all the raw data and correspondence on a special file, with duplicates used for daily work;

(*c*) retaining all working papers and drafts for future reference; it is of particular importance for the working papers to indicate what assumptions have been made in subdividing particular items of expenditure.

Specification of terms of reference

As mentioned in Chapter 3, in countries where a detailed health plan exists, objectives that can be evaluated in financial terms can be extracted. In the absence of such a plan, the survey team, before they begin their research, should ask for specific terms of reference which will depend on the size of the survey and may cover:

(1) national health objectives (including policy declarations relating to principles of international health policy such as primary health care);

(2) any further research objectives, developing the above in greater detail;

(3) the subdivisions of health care regarded as particulary policy-relevant;

(4) sources of finance that should be given special attention for policy formation (e.g., compulsory health insurance, foreign aid, the private sector);

(5) assumptions to be made about the future availability of funds in the public sector;

(6) any relevant policy developments (e.g., decisions to build further hospitals, however financed, or to extend the coverage of compulsory health insurance);

(7) any questions of major concern, for example, equity in the distribution of particular health resources (such as manpower for hospital facilities) between geographical areas or groups of the population (such as children, the aged, shanty town dwellers).

Specification of research objectives and data organization

Chapter 3 listed the types of information needed to meet particular objectives. Before the collection of data is begun, some of the summary tables should be designed to show, in visual form, the intended output from the data collection process. As an illustration, three models are presented. Tables 1 and 2 show models for analysing major expenditure categories and sources of finance over a four-year period. Table 3 gives a model for expenditure, by sources of finance, over a one-year period. These models show recurrent expenditure; similar tables will be needed for capital expenditure. In addition, two model summary tables of recurrent expenditure, by major sources of finance, used at a workshop on health sector financing surveys, are shown later, in Tables 11 and 12.

Once the specific research objectives are clarified, the data collection phase of the survey can begin.

Table 1. Recurrent expenditure for health over
a 4-year period, e.g., 1979-1982 (model)

Area of expenditure	Current prices (million NCU[a])				% change (1979 = 100%)		
	1979	1980	1981	1982	1980	1981	1982
Personal health care							
Institutional health care							
Ambulatory health services							
Special health programmes							
Health-related activities							
Support services (training, management, research and others)							
Total							
Primary health care (as part of total health expenditure)							
Total							

[a] NCU = national currency unit.

Table 2. Sources of finance for recurrent expenditure on health over a 4-year period, e.g., 1979–1982 (model)

Source of finance	Current prices (million NCU[a])				% share			
	1979	1980	1981	1982	1979	1980	1981	1982
Total health sector								
Government								
Compulsory health insurance								
Voluntary health insurance								
Private employers								
Local donations								
Private households								
External cooperation (official)								
External cooperation (non-official)								
Total					100	100	100	100
Primary health care (as part of total health sector)								
Government								
Compulsory health insurance								
Voluntary health insurance								
Private employers								
Local donations								
Private households								
External cooperation (official)								
External cooperation (non-official)								
Total					100	100	100	100

[a] NCU = national currency unit.

Table 3. Recurrent expenditure for health (million NCU^a) by sources of finance for any one year (model)

Area of expenditure	Public					Private				External cooperation	
	Ministry of health	Other govt. dept.	Local govt.	Compulsory health insurance	Private health insurance	Industry	Local donations (cash)	Private households	Donated labour	Official	Non-official
Personal health services											
Institutional health care											
Ambulatory health services											
Special health programmes											
Health-related activities											
Training, management, research and other health care services											
Total											
Primary health care (as part of total health expenditure)											
Total											

^{a} NCU = national currency unit.

CHAPTER 5

Data collection

Researchers should try to work from existing information and accounting systems, even if these were not designed for the current purpose and would need considerable adjustment. Rough estimates of data are often satisfactory for most purposes, providing they are made on some rational basis. An informed "guesstimate" is better than a large hole in a table of figures. The basis for "guesstimates" should be carefully recorded in working papers.

In collecting and processing data there are three critical principles:

(1) to ensure that all major items of finance and expenditure are included;

(2) to use figures for expenditure actually incurred rather than finance budgeted (which may not have been allocated or, if allocated, not spent);

(3) to avoid any double counting of money transferred from one source of finance to another before it is spent, which thus appears in more than one account.

In the sections that follow, the problems of obtaining and handling data for each source of finance are examined in turn. [1]

Ministry of health

While ministries normally receive the bulk of their funds from the ministry of finance, funds may also be received from external cooperation, special funds and charitable donations.

---

[1] Checklists of potential sources of information are given at the end of this chapter (pages 65–67) and further examples of related information are included in Annex 1.

The layout of the budget may consist only of a breakdown into such items as personnel, supplies and equipment, transport, and training. Two model tables are included, one for recurrent and one for capital expenditure, to show one of the ways in which data suitable for policy analysis can be organized (Tables 4 and 5).

The main sources of data are likely to be the recurrent and capital accounts of the ministry, government annual statements of accounts, reports of the ministry and similar documents. The aggregated data will normally have to be disaggregated with the help of raw data obtained from other sources (for example, information on the number, type and size of facilities run by the ministry; the number and category of personnel working in particular units; estimates from officials responsible for allocating supplies, e.g., drugs, between units at regional and/or central level).

The danger of *double counting* has already been mentioned. The suggested procedure is for the expenditure to be shown under the initial source of finance but also on the transfer line if it is a grant to another listed source of finance used in the study—e.g., a grant or subsidy to local government or missions that will spend it on their health activities. At the same time an entry should be made on a working sheet entitled "Notes about transfers" (Table 6). This will ensure that such expenditures will appear in the ministry of health column in the summary tables for the whole health sector, with an indication of their use.

The same principle applies to fees charged to patients by health services (hospitals, health centres or posts) run by the ministry, which will appear as revenue of the ministry. These amounts should also be recorded in the "Notes about transfers". The initial source of finance will be "Direct private payments for health services"; the type of expenditure will be "District hospitals", and it will appear as such in the final summary tables (see Table 11). Similarly some recurrent expenditure of the ministry of health may be financed by external cooperation. A careful check on the true original source of finance will identify services or activities financed from other than ministry sources. Once the table has been completed, the total should be transferred to the health sector summary table.

The table recording ministry of health capital expenditure should include only the investments (mainly buildings and equipment) that are financed by the ministry itself. The sources of finance should be checked and all expenditure not financed from domestic funds should

Table 4. Recurrent expenditure of ministry of health (current prices, million NCU[a]) for any one year (model)[b]

Area of expenditure	Staff costs	Travel-ling	Council and conf.	Water & elec-tricity charges	Postal & tele-phone charges	Train-ing of village health workers	Subven-tion to mission hospi-tals	Medical & sur-gical equip-ment	Drugs & dress-ings	Food for pa-tients	Training courses for nurses	Other (specify)	Total
National referral hosp.													
General hospital 1													
General hospital 2													
General hospital 3													
General hospital 4													
Long-stay hospital													
Mental hospital													
Communicable disease unit													
Sanitation unit													
Nutrition unit													
Health education													
Occupational health unit													
MCH-FP unit[c]													
Central lab. service													
Transport													
HQ administration													
Training—doctors, dentists													
Training—other health staff													
Medical research													
Total													
Transfers													
Total													

a NCU = national currency unit.
b See reference 8.
c MCH-FP unit = maternal and child health—family planning unit.

Table 5. Capital expenditure of ministry of health (current prices, million NCU[a]) for any one year (model)[b]

Area of expenditure	Project 1	Project 2	Project 3	Project 4	Project 5	Project 6	Total
National referral hospital							
General hospital 1							
General hospital 2							
General hospital 3							
General hospital 4							
Long-stay hospital							
Mental hospital							
Communicable disease programme							
Sanitation programme							
Nutrition programme							
Health education programme							
Occupational health programme							
MCH-FP programme[c]							
Central lab. service							
Transport							
HQ administration							
Training—doctors, dentists							
Training—other health staff							
Medical research							
Total							
Transfers							
Total							

[a] NCU = national currency unit.
[b] See reference 8. The number of project columns can be expanded as required.
[c] MCH-FP programme = maternal and child health—family planning programme.

Table 6. Notes about transfers (model)[a]

Initial source of finance	Amount	Spending agency	Item of expenditure

[a] See reference 8.

be recorded in the "Notes about transfers" (a separate note is needed for "capital"). These will be inserted later under the respective sources of finance. The reason for this procedure is to show external cooperation (or foreign aid) as a separate source of finance; national case studies in a number of countries have found a high proportion of health investments funded from external sources. The capital expenditure table should be completed on a similar basis to that for recurrent expenditure. The importance of obtaining information on the future recurrent costs caused by investments has already been mentioned.

Other ministries and local government

Other ministries

In most countries there are health expenditures incurred by departments other than the ministry of health. For example, buildings for health purposes may be provided by the ministry of public works. The ministry of defence may provide health services for members of the armed forces, and the department responsible for prisons for prisoners. The ministry of agriculture may provide veterinary services for the protection of human health and subsidies to basic foods. The ministry of education may provide health services for schoolchildren and pay for

43

the specialized education and training of health personnel. The ministry responsible for social welfare may provide medical care for residents of social welfare institutions. The ministry responsible for community development may pay for certain types of health education and other health promotional activities, in some cases for food relief programmes for destitutes. Nationalized transport undertakings, such as railways or airlines, may provide health services for their employees. What is important is to undertake a really thorough examination of the capital and recurrent accounts for all ministries, as health-related expenditure may be found in totally unexpected places. The key figures are not the money budgeted or voted but the money *actually spent* and it is these figures that should be entered in the relevant worksheets (see Tables 7 and 8).

While the lines and the headings of columns in Tables 7 and 8 are self-explanatory, and the identification of health-related expenditures should not be difficult, some special problems need discussion.

Ministry of public works

If this ministry is responsible not only for the construction of buildings for health but also for their maintenance, it may be found that detailed records are not kept of the actual expenses incurred on the upkeep of particular buildings. One way of making estimates is by assuming that costs are proportional to the floor areas of facilities.

The cost of water supplies used for commercial and industrial purposes should not be included. The cost of all water used for domestic consumption might be regarded as spent for "health" reasons if it would take too much effort to estimate that part of the cost of water supply projects which is undertaken specifically for the provision of safe drinking-water (*18*).

Ministry of agriculture

It is suggested that meat inspection should be classified under "Sanitation" costs, while expenditures on the control of rabies, brucellosis, tsetse fly, etc., should be classified under "Communicable disease control". The costs of special nutritional programmes may appear among the expenditures of this ministry.

Ministry of education

Health services for schoolchildren usually include immunizations, health screening programmes, eye or dental examinations and treat-

44

Table 7. Current expenditure (current prices, million NCU[a]) of other ministries (model)[b]

Area of expenditure	Ministry							Total
	Public works	Defence	Mineral resources	Agriculture	Education	Transport	Local gov.	
Teaching/national referral hospitals								
General hospitals								
Long-stay hospitals								
Mental hospitals								
Other institutions (specify)								
Services abroad								
Health centre/clinic with medical staff								
Health centre/clinic with paramed. nursing staff								
Health posts with community health workers only								
Private practitioners								
Indigenous health practitioners								
Private dental services								
Retail outlets (drugs and dressings)								
Other private sources (specify)								
Communicable disease control								
Domestic water supply								
Sanitation								
Nutrition programmes								
Health education programmes								
Occupational health services								
Other programmes (specify)								
Central laboratory service								
Transport								
Headquarters administration								
Training—doctors, dentists								
Training—other health staff								
Medical research								
Other services (specify)								
Total								
Transfers								
Total								

[a] NCU = national currency unit.　[b] See reference 8.

45

Table 8. Capital expenditure (million NCU[a]) of other ministries (model)[b]

Area of expenditure	Ministry								Total
	Public works	Defence	Mineral resources	Agriculture	Education	Transport	Local gov.	Other (specify)	
Teaching/national referral hospitals									
General hospitals									
Long-stay hospitals									
Mental hospitals									
Other institutions (specify)									
Health centre/clinic with medical staff									
Health centre/clinic with paramed./nursing staff									
Health posts with community health workers only									
Private practitioners									
Private dental services									
Other private sources (specify)									
Communicable disease control									
Domestic water supply									
Sanitation									
Nutrition programmes									
Health education programmes									
Occupational health services									
Other programmes (specify)									
Central laboratory service									
Transport									
Headquarters administration									
Training—doctors, dentists									
Training—other health staff									
Medical research									
Other services (specify)									
Total									
Transfers									
Total									

[a] NCU = national currency unit.   [b] See reference 8.

ment, and the dispensing of certain drugs. If data are not available to permit a breakdown, it may be helpful to sample several villages and school districts to ascertain the proportion of education expenditure devoted to particular health services. This proportion could then be applied to the total amount spent by the ministry of education.

In many countries, the cost of training physicians appears in the accounts of this ministry, while the training of other health personnel is the responsibility of the ministry of health. The cost of general education of health personnel, prior to specialized training for health, should not be included. An important expenditure category is fellowships for studies abroad, often financed by foreign donors. Unit costs by type and location of training, compared with the cost of training in the home country, may provide important information for evaluation.

Ministry of transport

In some countries, the running costs of the vehicles of the ministry of health are borne by this ministry or a similar agency. If separate accounts are not kept of the expenditure on these vehicles, the percentage of the ministry of health's share of the total number of vehicles can be used for calculation of the health-related expenditure of this ministry.

Following the review of health-related expenditure of all ministries, it is again necessary to check the sources of finance. Only expenditure from domestic funds should be included; expenditure financed from other sources (e.g., external cooperation) should be recorded in the "Notes about transfers" and shown in the appropriate column of the sector summary tables.

Local government

The management of public health services has been decentralized in many countries and the responsibility given, for example, to town and district councils. The responsibility may vary from running health centres and health posts to carrying out and supervising refuse collection, sanitary inspection, etc. Sometimes, information on these expenditures can be collected at the central level of government, from the ministry of health or a separate ministry such as a ministry of local government. When figures on local expenditures cannot be obtained from one central point, they will have to be collected from the local authorities themselves. If there are no separate health departments within the local authorities, it may be necessary to allocate some overhead costs, particularly for administration. If the number of local units is large, sampling can be used to reduce the time and resources needed to collect the information. Table 9 shows one possible way of organizing the data for each local authority.

The task is to complete the tables with data found in the expenditure accounts of each district and town council and, with the help of information from other sources (e.g., a list showing the number and type of facilities run by the council; salary scales; expenditure on drugs by type of facility), to work out the details by health centre, health post, expenditure on sanitation, etc.

As in the case of the central ministries, it is necessary to check upon the initial sources of finance. If part of the current revenue of councils is received from the ministry of finance, this should be considered as the local government's own source of finance; on the other hand, a grant from the ministry of health budget should be shown by transfer as ministry of health expenditure in the summary tables.

Local authorities may also charge patients for health services; such revenue should be transferred and shown as "Direct private payment for health services".

The procedure for capital expenditure of local authorities is similar to that described for recurrent expenditure. The totals, for both expenditures, will be entered in the appropriate column of the sector summary tables.

Compulsory health insurance (social security)

An increasing number of countries throughout the world (about 70 in 1975) have established compulsory insurance programmes which may finance health care for a section of the population. In poorer developing countries, the proportion of the population covered tends to be relatively small, as such schemes are normally confined to persons with a regular cash income. The expenditures of social security programmes can, however, be substantial (particularly in Latin America), and such programmes are often quite separate from those run by the ministry of health. In identifying these expenditures it is important to take care to exclude from the amounts recorded as paid to providers

Table 9. Current expenditure of local government (model)[a]

Area of expenditure	Staff costs	Drugs & dressings	Transport	Administration	Health inspection & sanitation	Other (specify)	Total
Teaching/national referral hospitals							
General hospitals							
Long-stay hospitals							
Mental hospitals							
Other institutions (specify)							
Services abroad							
Health centre/clinic with medical staff							
Health centre/clinic with paramed./nursing staff							
Health posts with community health workers only							
Private practitioners							
Indigenous health practitioners							
Private dental services							
Retail outlets (drugs and dressings)							
Other private sources (specify)							
Communicable disease control							
Domestic water supply							
Sanitation							
Nutrition programmes							
Health education programmes							
Occupational health services							
Other programmes (specify)							
Central laboratory service							
Transport							
Headquarters administration							
Training—doctors, dentists							
Training—other health staff							
Medical research							
Other services (specify)							
Total							
Transfers							
Total							

[a] See reference 8.

49

of health services cash benefits paid to sick persons as well as partial or total reimbursements of their medical expenses.

Social security systems often receive contributions from the government. In the summary tables, such contributions should be counted as the expenditure of central government and not of compulsory health insurance.

Compulsory health insurance schemes generally have well developed records from which tables can be prepared similar to those used for ministries. In some cases capital expenditure as well as recurrent expenditure may be found, and where this occurs it should be separately recorded. The appropriate administrative costs should also be included. The disaggregation of expenditures (for example the amounts paid for particular curative services), classified by the providers of these services, may require a special procedure for estimation.

If the role of social security is very small in the expenditures of a country, it may not be worth treating it as an independent source of financing, and the funds could be regarded as those of employers, employees and government.

Voluntary health insurance

Schemes may be operated by friendly or mutual benefit societies, trade unions and other non-profit-making groups or by private profit-making insurance corporations. Private insurance can be bought by employers, individuals or groups. Total contributions from all sources should be included in this category, even though part of the contributions may be used to pay for administration, sales promotion, profit or surplus as well as to pay for or reimburse health care costs. Any cash benefits to the sick should be excluded.

Schemes of this kind are not extensive in most developing countries. They normally cover only the higher income groups. But wider programmes of different kinds may be found, possibly associated with agricultural cooperatives, particularly in South-East Asia. Some of the "grass roots" insurance arrangements of rural communities which pay for primary health care are mentioned in Chapter 7.

Data obtained from insurance agencies, relating both to recurrent and capital expenditure, should be entered in the appropriate columns of the summary tables.

Missions

This is a category of health service provider which may be unknown in some countries and very important in others. Originally emissaries of various European and North American religious bodies, combining evangelical and medical work in Africa, Asia and Latin America, their activities were funded from what would now be classified as "foreign aid". However, this pattern has changed in the last two or three decades; the flow of external funds has decreased and many governments of newly independent countries give subsidies to mission hospitals and clinics.

Missions generally keep formal accounts. Data collection may be facilitated if there is an umbrella organization, for example, an "association of missions" with centralized information. The records will normally provide such data as the cost of staff, drugs, transport and administration by particular units; the total should be shown in the appropriate column of the summary tables. Capital expenditure may also be incurred.

Checking the sources of income is again important. Besides funds from the religious bodies abroad and government subsidies, the missions may receive local donations and collect fees for health services from patients. Usually none of the revenues is earmarked for any special purpose, and the proportion of the total income used in each area can be regarded as the proportion of expenditure in each area. The amount of government subsidy should be recorded in the "Notes about transfers" and shown as government expenditure. In turn, the amount received from other private sources should be noted as a "Transfer" payment; similarly, fees paid for services in mission hospitals should be noted as "Transfers" and entered in the "Direct private payments for health services" column for "District hospitals" in the summary tables. Similarly, a mission hospital may receive funds from private foreign aid; such an item should be entered in the "Notes about transfers" and shown in the "External cooperation, non-official" column of the summary tables.

Employers

Factories, mines and agricultural estates may provide health care for their employees, either directly or through a welfare fund. Certain categories of employers—for example, those employing more than 500 workers—may be legally required to provide first-aid, hospital services and occupational health services. Sometimes groups of small firms in an area jointly finance such services. Some central authority or umbrella organization, e.g., ministry of labour or industry, ministry of health, or an association of plantations, may have records of this expenditure. The services provided may range from health services proper to health services and some indirect or non-personal health services—for example, mine safety (or accident prevention). In such cases, a table may contain the following areas of expenditure: general hospitals, sanitation, occupational health, transport and other (administration).

When checking the sources of finance under the heading "Industry", account should be taken of the payments made by individuals in the form of fees. These amounts should be noted and transferred to the column "Direct private payments" in the summary tables. Similarly grants may be received from central or local government.

The capital expenditures of health services run by industry may be funded from other than industrial sources, for example, from "External cooperation, official" or a grant from the ministry of health. These items should be noted as transfers and included under "Foreign aid, official" or "Ministry of health" in the summary tables.

Local voluntary bodies

Voluntary bodies, such as the Red Cross, Rotary Club, women's groups, etc., may contribute money, services or donations in kind to the health service. The nature of these contributions is relatively easy to identify, but collecting information about them can present problems. In larger developing countries, there may be hundreds of such bodies or organizations, and not all keep formal accounts: the secretaries of the major ones may need to be interviewed or contacted by correspondence.

The sources of finance of voluntary bodies must be identified with care. Only a small percentage of their budget may come from philanthropic donations. Some donations, as mentioned, may be in the form of voluntary work, the value of which should be roughly estimated at market wage rates. A part of the budget may come from government subsidies (usually from the ministry of health) or from foreign aid and should be shown as a transfer. Private payments made for the use of ambulances to transport patients to or from hospitals are also often a source of revenue for the Red Cross.

Direct private payments

Direct payments from individuals or households for health services generally represent a large proportion of the total expenditure of the health sector, although this fact is not always recognized. It is suggested that the definition of health expenditure should not include:

(a) personal expenditure on food, housing or clothing;

(b) the value of working time lost by seeking health care;

(c) the private cost of transport and accommodation when seeking health care. [1]

The last two items are clearly relevant to a full economic appraisal which includes social costs. Moreover, travel cost, travel time and waiting time are important in considering the question of equity. Their exclusion is suggested simply because of the practical problems of obtaining data.

Information on individual payment for health services can be obtained either from households or from providers of services. Data on consumer expenditures are often collected in periodic general or specific household surveys. Such surveys may only cover urban areas and not all expenditures on health may be included. As surveys of this kind are costly, they tend to be infrequent.

Perhaps the most practical way of collecting these data is from small surveys of the money received over the year by the main providers of health care—private physicians, dentists, nurses and traditional practitioners of different kinds, as well as hospitals and pharmacies. Experience has shown that most providers are willing to cooperate, providing they are assured that their individual returns will be kept confidential and only used for producing an aggregate estimate. Care needs to be taken to avoid double counting (e.g., with compulsory or private health insurance) and to add in any items already recorded in the "Notes on transfers".

---

[1] The payments made for transport by providers of care, e.g., the fees paid for use of Red Cross ambulances should be counted.

Expenditure on hospitals, clinics and health posts

Payments to private hospitals and other facilities (if any) can be ascertained from their accounts. In some countries, the turnover from nursing homes can be obtained from returns made for business turnover tax purposes. Where accounts are not centrally available a questionnaire may need to be circulated, possibly stratified by size of insitution. The questionnaire shown on page 55 is based on one used in one study.

Expenditure on private practitioners

Average gross receipts per practitioner can be estimated with the help of professional associations and doctors working for the government; information might also be obtained from government tax collection departments, though in this case earnings may be understated. The average per practitioner can then be multiplied by the number of personnel in private clinical practice, adjusting for those in semi-retirement and allowing for those partly in public and partly in private practice. For smaller groups of professionals well-informed guesses may have to be made.

In some cases, the consistency of different estimates can be checked by comparing different sources of information. For example, the amounts paid from public funds to private practitioners may be known and those made by private insurance, industry, foreign aid, etc. The total of these payments can be deducted from the total estimated gross earnings of private practitioners (estimated on the basis of data from professional associations) to give an estimate of private direct payments. These data can be compared with estimates derived from consumer expenditure surveys.

Expenditure on traditional practitioners

It is difficult to estimate the earnings of traditional practitioners; many of them practice part-time, particularly traditional birth attendants, and they may receive substantial payments in kind (e.g., sheep, goats or chickens). They are also geographically widely dispersed and thus difficult to survey. Estimates have, however, been made for some countries, showing that the expenditure is considerable. For example, in Botswana, expenditures on the services of about 8000 traditional practitioners and 1000 traditional birth attendants were estimated from

SURVEY ON HEALTH EXPENDITURE—PRIVATE SECTOR HOSPITALS

1. Name and address:_____

2. Facilities available (delete whichever is not applicable):
   (a) Outpatient treatments   Yes/No
   (b) In-patient treatments   Yes/No
   (c) If answer to (b) above is "Yes" give the bed strength under each category:

	1979	1980	1981
(1) medical			
(2) surgical			
(3) paediatric			
(4) maternity			

   (d) Operating theatre   Yes/No
   (e) X-ray   Yes/No
   (f) Laboratory   Yes/No
   (g) Dental surgery   Yes/No
   (h) Channel consultation   Yes/No
   (i) Approximate floor space (in m²)

	1979	1980
(1) indoors		
(2) out-of-doors		

3. Employees and their remuneration (annual salaries, wages and other personal allowances, except travelling expenses, for the year 1979):

	Total number		Total remuneration	
	Permanent	Part-time	Permanent	Part-time
(a) Medical consultants				
(b) Physicians/house officers				
(c) Radiologists				
(d) Assistant/registered medical practitioners				
(e) Matrons, sisters, nurses				
(f) Technicians				
(g) Unskilled and semi-skilled labour (including attendants, drivers, cooks and labourers)				

4. Performance:

	Annual total			Daily average		
	1979	1980	1981	1979	1980	1981
(a) Number of outpatients						
(1) through own clinics						
(2) through channel consultations						
(b) Number of in-patients						
(c) Number of surgical patients						
(d) Number of maternity cases						
(e) Number of in-patient nights				NA	NA	NA

5. Finance: please submit copies of annual balance sheets and income/expenditure statements for 1979 and 1980.

a rural income distribution survey, a report on primary health care in one district, and the national accounts of the country. In many cases, ministries of health have considerable knowledge of the number and earnings of different categories of traditional healers. Studies by medical anthropologists and others may also have yielded estimates of the average or aggregate earnings of traditional healers in other countries. In India, where Ayurvedic medicine is well organized, information may be available from societies of practitioners; in China, most traditional doctors have been incorporated into the official health care system and simply receive a salary; patients' payments contribute to the cost of operating the total health care programme. In some countries, consumer expenditure surveys specifically ask about expenditure on traditional services as a separate identifiable item. This can form the basis of an estimate of an acceptable accuracy.

Expenditure on drugs and other health-related supplies

Purchases of drugs, herbs and first-aid supplies by private individuals at retail outlets are generally substantial even when free or very low-priced drugs are made available by the official health services. Pharmaceutical companies or special market survey organizations have often collected sales information from pharmacies, drug stores or food stores where medicines are sold.

For estimating this category of expenditure, interviews with selected pharmacies, discussions with the chief pharmacist of the ministry of health, and information from industry-sponsored or government-sponsored household surveys should be used when available. An alternative method is to work from trade statistics on the importation of medicines plus any local production. If this latter method is used, the value of drugs paid for from public funds, industry, etc., will need to be subtracted from the totals.

Expenditure on water fees

Water supply agencies or parastatal bodies, particularly in towns and cities, are financed by private payments from households or individuals. Information can normally be obtained from the accounts of water supply organizations.

Self-help and other private sources

This column of the summary tables can be used for data on the health-related self-help activities of particular villages or local communities. For example, a group of villages may construct and run a maternity centre or operate a village health post. Data collection will require contact with a large number of groups, unless some central source of information is available.

Private donations and charity, whether for missions or other purposes, should appear in this column as "Transfers".

External cooperation

Funds may be multilateral from UNICEF, UNDP, WHO or another international agency, or bilateral from individual countries. Financial cooperation may be channelled to a central authority such as the ministry of finance or bureau of planning, which coordinates foreign aid, or to a particular ministry such as the ministry of health or education, or directly to other institutions or agencies such as mission health services. Sometimes cooperation takes the form of donated equipment, supplies, manpower or fellowships.

The World Bank and other, similar development banks are the source of many loans for health-related projects, such as the construction of water supply systems or health centres.

In some countries, a yearly report describes all development projects assisted from external sources. Further documents may need to be consulted to clarify whether a particular item should be classified as part of the health sector and precisely what it was for. For some purposes it may be useful to show expenditure categories by major donors. In the summary tables, external cooperation is divided only into "official" and "non-official". "Official" means funding from national governments, irrespective of whether it is channelled through bilateral or multilateral organizations. "Non-official" external cooperation means the rest of external cooperation—mainly funds from private foundations and the value of the work of foreign volunteers.

It is important to establish whether the data assembled in a report are in the form of commitments (funds budgeted) or disbursements (money handed over by the donor but not necessarily spent) or cover amounts actually spent. It is the latter information that is required. It may well be necessary to go back to each donor and ask for a special return. This procedure, though laborious, has the advantage of identifying grants outside the public sector—for example, to voluntary bodies. The information requested should cover whether the grant or loan was for capital or recurrent expenditure, to whom the grant was made, and on what the money was spent. Care should be taken to include all potential donors in the enquiry—not only international organizations and banks (e.g., World Bank, Asian Development Bank, European Economic Community) but each national aid agency which may have given aid to the health sector.

One way in which data may be organized is shown in Table 10. In the first column, transfers recorded earlier in a table of notes on transfers are brought together. Separate tables may be needed for aid to government and for aid to other agencies listed (voluntary associations, employers, etc.). In each case, capital and recurrent items should be handled separately.

Additional possible sources of information technical cooperation are the personnel records of the ministry of health and other ministries and major institutions. These records may show the number and category of health workers, the working place (for example, a general hospital), source of funding (foreign aid, official), type of funding (fully, partly, etc.) and their salary. Average salaries can be worked out for each category and multiplied by the number of personnel. Expatriates may receive additional payments from the host government; such emoluments should be counted under the ministry of health (or other ministry) and not under external cooperation.

Conventions differ among countries on the extent to which external cooperation received for government services is shown in government accounts. Some gifts in kind, including large ones like the construction of a whole hospital, may not be included. Thus it is important to clarify which expenditures financed by external cooperation have been incorporated in government accounts, and are thus shown as government expenditure, and which have not. External cooperation included as government expenditure should be deducted from the expenditure of the particular government department, recorded on a transfer sheet and ultimately shown as external cooperation.

Expenditure on **training programmes** not accounted for through government accounts, should be included where financed by external cooperation (e.g., cost of courses and workshops on nutrition, sanita-

Table 10. Contribution of official external cooperation to health sector current expenditure (model)[a]

Area of expenditure	Expend. identi-fied previously[b]	Technical cooperation	Training activities	Supplies in kind	Direct provision of helath services	Total
Teaching/national referral hospitals						
General hospitals						
Long-stay hospitals						
Mental hospitals						
Other institutions (specify)						
Services abroad						
Health centre/clinic with medical staff						
Health centre/clinic with paramed./nursing staff						
Health posts with community health workers only						
Private practitioners						
Indigenous health practitioners						
Private dental services						
Retail outlets (drugs and dressings)						
Other private sources (specify)						
Communicable disease control						
Domestic water supply						
Sanitation						
Nutrition programmes						
Health education programmes						
Occupational health services						
Other programmes (specify)						
Central laboratory service						
Transport						
Headquarters administration						
Training—doctors, dentists						
Training—other health staff						
Medical research						
Other services (specify)						
Total						
Transfers						
Total						

[a] See reference 8.

[b] Recorded in notes on transfers.

tion, equipment maintenance, etc.). The column of the table should be correctly chosen, e.g., if the training is clearly in nutrition or sanitation, such entries should be on those lines, rather than on "Training—other health workers".

A separate table may be required for **fellowships** abroad, showing the type and site of training, the number of students, the unit cost of a fellowship, a total column and the source of funding (e.g., official or non-official external cooperation). In Table 10, expenditure on fellowships is included with the cost of other training programmes.

Supplies in kind may be valued according to the prevailing local practice, e.g., national retail value, or the original price paid by the donor or world market prices. This category will include any donations of the World Food Programme for certain categories of the population (children, the very poor, the aged, or people living in catastrophy areas) and contraceptives distributed by the International Planned Parenthood Federation.

Direct provision of health services. Here any other health services financed by foreign aid other than those of missions should be listed.

Separate tables need to be completed on similar lines for recurrent expenditure and for capital expenditure and the totals transferred to the appropriate columns of summary tables of the type shown in Tables 11 and 12. Additional tables for each category of source of finance, with the same classification of expenditure as shown in Table 11, might be prepared to cover past years to facilitate the analysis of trends.

Further details on data collection are contained in teaching material (entitled "*Teaching modules for health sector financing surveys*") prepared for a two-week training course.[1]

Financial flows

While identifying the major sources of finance for the health sector it is also useful to collect information on the flow of money, i.e., the process of financing. For example, in the government sector the ministry of finance allots money collected in taxes and from other sources to the ministry of health and other ministries for health purposes; the central ministries may give money to different levels of local government and ultimately a health institution spends the money on

---

[1] Further information on the teaching modules is given by Griffith & Mills (8).

Table 11. Total health sector current expenditure (model) [a]

Area of expenditure	Ministry of health	Other ministries	Local government	Other state bodies	Missions	Industry	Local voluntary bodies	Direct private payments for health services	Insurance	Self-help and other private resources	Foreign aid, official	Foreign aid, private	Total
Teaching/national referral hospitals													
General hospitals													
Long-stay hospitals													
Mental hospitals													
Other institutions (specify)													
Services abroad													
Health centre/clinic with medical staff													
Health centre/clinic with paramed./ nursing staff													
Health posts with community health workers only													
Private practitioners													
Indigenous health practitioners													
Private dental services													
Retail outlets (drugs and dressings)													
Other private sources (specify)													
Communicable disease control													
Domestic water supply													
Sanitation													
Nutrition programmes													
Health education programmes													
Occupational health services													
Other programmes (specify)													
Central laboratory service													
Transport													
Headquarters administration													
Training—doctors, dentists													
Training—other health staff													
Medical research													
Other services (specify)													
Total													
Transfers													
Total													

[a] See reference 8.

Table 12. Total health sector capital expenditure (model)[a]

Area of expenditure	Ministry of health	Other ministries	Local government	Other state bodies	Missions	Industry	Local voluntary bodies	Direct private payments for health services	Insurance	Self-help and other private resources	Foreign aid, official	Foreign aid, private	Total
Teaching/national referral hospitals													
General hospitals													
Long-stay hospitals													
Mental hospitals													
Other institutions (specify)													
Health centre/clinic with medical staff													
Health centre/clinic with paramed./ nursing staff													
Health posts with community health workers only													
Private practitioners													
Private dental services													
Other private sources (specify)													
Communicable disease control													
Domestic water supply													
Sanitation													
Nutrition programmes													
Health education programmes													
Occupational health services													
Other programmes (specify)													
Central laboratory service													
Transport													
Headquarters administration													
Training—doctors, dentists													
Training—other health staff													
Medical research													
Other services (specify)													
Total													
Transfers													
Total													

[a] See reference 8.

services. Or external cooperation may flow through central government to local government and from there to charitable bodies. Or employers may pay towards insurance schemes for their workers, which in turn pay for the health care of the insured workers (and their families).

The methods of data collection recommended in this chapter provided for an entry line for "Transfers" for each major source of finance and recommended the recording of each transfer item in "Notes about transfers". In addition, an attempt should be made to obtain information on the flow of major categories of funds from source to final spender, including the intermediate institutions or agencies and the time taken for funds to reach their final destination. The process can be illustrated visually by simple flowcharts which can be helpful when the time comes to draw up recommendations.

Sources of information on the flow of funds could be the managers of funds at different levels of government, personnel of health institutions dealing with budget, personnel of external cooperation agencies, government reports and accounts, and health services research studies. Interviews with knowledgeable persons may provide valuable information on how the method of financing affects, for example, the volume and type of services used.

A checklist of sources of finance, revenue and information and examples of related information are shown on pages 65–69 and examples of actual tables produced for a developing country are shown for illustration in Annex 1.

Small surveys and samples

Other types of information that will be required to supplement the financing data may not generally be available. The survey team may have to organize and undertake small sample surveys itself; on the other hand, the health planning unit of the ministry of health could undertake these routinely from time to time, since the information will be of general value for health planning. In the short term these could be simple, one-day or two-day random samples of particular facilities and activities; they would be cheap and easy to do, yet serve their purpose by giving the survey team additional insight into the operation of the health services, and thus provide a firmer basis for the interpretation of strictly financial data drawn from secondary sources. In the long term, special research projects could be undertaken.

Examples of this type of information are:

Time and motion studies	— different types of health manpower in one facility
	— same type of manpower in different facilities
Access to health services and facilities	— travelling distances and times for outpatients by types of facilities, by different areas
	— referrals to hospitals, number, types, distances
Use of medical supplies and equipment	— standard list of drugs
	— standard list of medical instruments
	— standard list of furniture/equipment for clinics
	— standard list of furniture/equipment for health posts
	— drug usage in different types of health facilities
	— vehicle usage, time and motion
	— main uses for food, electricity, water, gas, telephone, etc.
Use and cost of hospitals	— utilization rates, unit cost of services, alternatives to hospitalization (ambulatory care, home care, self-care), comparisons of costs per patient in different types of hospital (teaching versus general, etc.).

TENTATIVE CHECKLISTS OF SOURCES OF FINANCE, REVENUE AND INFORMATION

1. SOURCE OF FINANCE	ORIGINAL SOURCE OF REVENUE	INFORMATION SOURCE FOR ORIGINAL SOURCE OF REVENUE
Government Central (all ministries) State Local Municipal		General: government annual statement of accounts and budget; national accounts and reports of ministries (health, education, public works, central office of statistics, etc.)
	Direct taxes Income Profits Other	Tax office: interviews, annual reports
	Indirect taxes Sales tax	Ministry of finance: interviews, reports
	Customs duties Excise tax	Customs office: interviews, reports
	Property tax	Tax office: local government records; ministry of finance
	User tax	Ministry of finance; tax office
	Gambling/sports tax	Ministry of finance; tax office; state/regional treasuries
	Other External borrowing Royalties, rents Fines Licence fees Miscellaneous charges	Ministry of finance
	Transfers/grants	Ministry of finance annual statement of accounts; receiving ministry's budget
Compulsory/ voluntary health insurance	Employee contribution Employer contribution Government contribution User fees Special taxes Lottery receipts	Insurance agency annual reports, records and interviews

1. SOURCE OF FINANCE	ORIGINAL SOURCE OF REVENUE	INFORMATION SOURCE FOR ORIGINAL SOURCE OF REVENUE
External cooperation Official Non-official	External public revenue or private funds in the form of: grants, loans, training, supplies, personnel	Donor and receiving agencies: reports, interviews. National coordinating agency for foreign cooperation (ministry of finance, bureau of planning): comprehensive report
Charitable and voluntary organizations Missions Red Cross Other	Local fund-raising Government subsidy Foreign assistance	Annual reports and accounts; interviews; special requests
Industry and business Mines Plantations Farms Banks Railways Manufacturers	Operational revenue Fees for services Foreign assistance Local donations	Annual reports; income/expenditure statements; balance sheets, interviews; special requests; tax office
Private individuals	Income (agriculture, trade, etc.) Wages and salaries (cash, labour or material donated to health programmes)	Income, employment and household surveys; special research; tax office

2. HEALTH EXPENDITURE	INFORMATION SOURCE
Institutional health care Teaching hospitals General hospitals Long-stay hospitals Other institutions	Hospital budgets and accounts; ministry of health accounts, records and reports; hospital federation reports; interviews; studies, including products of health services research
Ambulatory health care Health centres with medical staff or with paramedical and nursing staff	National health development plans; records, reports of supervising authorities; sample surveys; household surveys; rural development reports
Health posts with community health workers	As for health centres; primary health care studies; donor agency reports (national and external)

2. HEALTH EXPENDITURE

	INFORMATION SOURCE
Private practitioners and private dental services	Ministry of health and tax office records; interviews; special research; reports of associations (of physicians, nurses, midwives)
Indigenous health practitioners	As for private practitioners (including associations which now exist in many developing countries)
Drugs	Trade statistics related to national drug production and sales; reports on annual drug importation; reports of ministry of health, pharmaceutical companies and special market survey organizations; household surveys; interviews with selected collaborating pharmacies, discussions with the chief pharmacist of the ministry of health
Other private services	Ministry of health; organizations; associations of providers

Special health programmes

Communicable disease control	Specific health care organizations
Health education	Ministries of health and education; non-governmental organizations, the media
Occupational health	Ministries of health and labour; trade unions; associations of manufacturers
Sanitation	Ministries of health, public works and planning; local authorities
Water supplies	As for sanitation; state bodies in charge of water supplies
Training of health personnel	Ministries of health and education; providers associations
Nutrition programmes	Ministries of agriculture, health and education; local authorities (or ministry of local government or interior)
Medical research	National medical research council; academy of sciences, universities research institutions; ministries of health and education; associations of researchers

EXAMPLES OF RELATED INFORMATION

TOPIC	POSSIBLE SOURCES
Distribution of income (geographically, by level of income, family size, level of education, etc.)	Special surveys: — income distribution — household expenditures — employment National development plan National accounts National commissions on salary increases
Population characteristics and distribution (geographical distribution of population, birth rates, death rates, fertility, etc.)	National statistics office Census report Medical statistics office Regional planning department National development plan
Distribution of employment (by salary/wage level, geographically, by education, etc.)	Employment surveys National development plan Reports on localization Census report
Access to health services and facilities (types and distribution of facilities, population coverage, services provided, etc.)	Ministry of health and other main providers: annual reports Reports on development projects Medical statistics, annual reports Special studies: — medical statistics — health planning — university research
Health manpower (by number, types, geographical distribution, salary scales, agency and facility distribution, etc.)	Establishment registers, ministries Personnel department, ministry of health Main providers, annual reports Annual recurrent estimates submissions Reports on localization Special requests where necessary
Distribution of household expenditures (personal and family expenditures on health services, medicines, etc.)	Surveys of household expenditure
Medical statistics	Medical statistics annual reports Main providers annual reports Special surveys: — household expenditures — private practitioners — traditional practitioners
Official plan and policy statements	Current national development plan Presidential addresses Budget introductory speeches Speeches by minister of health Ministry of health annual report Personal knowledge

TOPIC	POSSIBLE SOURCES
Direct and indirect taxes (tax scales, tax regulations, distribution of taxes by type of payee, by income level of payee, etc.)	Departments of taxes and customs, annual reports National development plan Special tax agencies: — health insurance — local government taxes Special requests
Trade statistics	Trade statistics and department of customs, annual reports
National accounts	National accounts (latest report) National accounts unit National development plan
State of the economy	Budget introductory speeches National development plan Presidential addresses Ministry of economic planning

CHAPTER 6

Primary health care

Definition

The evolution and main characteristics of the primary health care approach were described in the "Introduction". In principle, it is more than a programme or a set of programmes; its eight components cut across the totality of the health sector; it is not just the health care of rural people or that of dwellers in shanty towns. However, in some countries primary health care is considered in a narrower sense, as the level of health care at the periphery of a health system, or the activities performed at the point of contact between the health system and the community.

The precise definition of primary health care becomes important when politicians, donor agencies or public health administrators ask how much is spent or needs to be spent on it and how it can best be financed. Costing it in its broadest sense, which goes far beyond health care to include education, the availability of food, safe drinking-water, housing, and employment, i.e., almost everything meant by development, is obviously impracticable. Furthermore, even within the limits of basic health services, proper costing should begin by measuring the need which has to be met.

Information on the cost of primary health care, coupled with data on utilization, quality and extent of coverage and the extent of different sections of the population by different parts of the programme is needed to give a comprehensive description of the present situation. From this, plans can be made for development. It is proposed that a practical definition might include:

(1) all health care from the village or urban community level up to the health centre or first-line hospital;

(2) part of the cost of some vertical programmes, such as communi-

71

cable disease control or health education;

(3) the cost of domestic water supplies, sanitation, nutrition and any other activities regarded locally as part of primary health care (see Table 13).

Table 13. Recurrent expenditure on primary
health care over a 4-year period, e.g., 1979–1982 (model)

Area of expenditure	Current prices (million NCU[a])				% change (1979–100%)		
	1979	1980	1981	1982	1980	1981	1982
Health activities							
Health centres							
Health posts							
Private practitioners							
Indigenous health practitioners							
Private dental services							
Communicable disease control							
Health education							
Training							
Health-related activities							
Domestic water supply							
Sanitation							
Nutrition							
Activities to improve housing							
Total							

[a] NCU = national currency unit.

Ideally, at the national level, the following kinds of information would be required:

Expenditure on basic health services, including that on village health workers, a village dispensary run by a community, traditional practitioners of all kinds, a health post, a rural clinic, and a rural health centre used for the referral of patients needing medical care. Throughout this manual, a distinction needs to be made between capital expenditure (e.g., the construction of a building, purchase of durable equipment) and recurrent costs (salaries of personnel, cost of supplies including medicaments, maintenance of buildings and equipment, transport, and other charges such as water and electricity). For certain purposes it may be useful to break down total primary health care expenditure into such activities as maternal and child care or vaccination programmes, personal curative services and control of major categories of

72

diseases (e.g., diarrhoeal diseases, tuberculosis, and malaria), or health education.

Expenditure on water supply, sanitation and nutrition programmes aimed at the improvement of health.

Expenditure on training for primary health care. This covers training for all levels of health and other personnel. At the village level, training is needed in community leadership for village health workers and for general development personnel. At the intermediate level, training is required for future trainers and refresher training is needed for all health personnel (nurses staffing health posts, rural health centres, maternity centres) and physicians in order to prepare them for more community-oriented work. At the central level, reorientation is necessary for staff dealing with planning and management of the health sector to promote more equitable distribution of funds, the use of appropriate technologies, and other principles of primary health care.

Data collection

Many of the sources and methods described in Chapter 5 can be used to obtain the information, even if it is only possible to establish the order of magnitude of national expenditures on primary health care and the sources of finance. In most countries, there are studies, reports and pilot projects on primary health care which provide information on costs and funding. Expenditures of publicly financed rural health facilities are generally known locally or centrally. Where aggregated data are not available, a combination of the following methods of producing estimates may be used.

Expenditure on manpower

Estimates are required of salaries and wages of health personnel employed in primary health care areas. For the public sector the number and geographical deployment of personnel and their salary scales are generally known by the ministry of health. For other personnel, data from studies or records of some central bureaux (e.g., statistics bureau, coordination office of religious missions, records of donor agencies) may be used and, if necessary, extrapolated for the whole country. The salaries and number of employees working in domestic water supply or nutrition programmes should be known by the ministries supervising these programmes. From these data, the cost of the manpower component of primary health care and its urban/rural distribution can be calculated. What is urban and what is rural has, of course, to be defined. Estimates of the value of donated labour can be made in monetary terms by using prevalent wage rates.

Estimates of expenditure on private and/or traditional practitioners were discussed in Chapter 5 (pages 54–56). An increasing number of countries collect information on the number and kind of practitioners, the number of patients visiting these practitioners, and the order of magnitude of the fees charged to patients, usually per episode of sickness. The rates charged by healers can also be found out by asking small samples of patients. Payments in kind can be valued according to the market value of the "reward", e.g., a chicken, etc. In this way, the income of practitioners can be estimated for an area or region, and total estimates made for a country. Newly-formed associations usually attempt to carry out a national census of traditional healers, as the knowledge of their geographical location and specialty can be helpful in planning future health service coverage of the population.

In many countries, volunteers make a substantial contribution to primary health care. This work should be identified and valued. It includes not only the provision of services but the staffing of village pharmacies and the operation of informal health insurance systems on a cooperative basis.

Expenditure on training

The types of activity and their costs are usually known by the training units of the ministry of health or the ministries responsible for water supply, sanitation and nutrition programmes; in addition, reports of selected local authorities and external cooperation agencies can be examined to make sure that all training costs incurred in the country are included. As in the case of salaries, it is important to identify the intended beneficiaries of training, i.e., where the trainees are intended to work.

Supplies and equipment

National data are usually available on public expenditure on drugs, broken down by geographical region of the country. The value of drugs used by urban hospitals is usually recorded separately. From data of this kind, it is possible to calculate the cost not only of drugs but of other supplies used in urban and rural health services; the calculations can be checked against special studies analysing the cost of certain health facilities or dealing with selected primary health care-type projects. Rough estimates of the value of traditional remedies and of supplies used in, for example, mission dispensaries also need to be included.

Other costs

Under this heading, the maintenance costs of buildings and equipment, and transport, water and electricity charges incurred in basic health facilities or by primary health care workers are included. Rough estimates related to different types of facilities are usually available and can be used for estimating the total. The value of drugs and equipment used by village health workers is often known from project budgets, donor agency reports, etc.

Investments

In Chapter 5, different sources of information on capital expenditures on health and ways of organizing the data were described. The definition of primary health care used for the study should be applied to these data. For example, if it has been decided that health facilities in rural areas, from a village dispensary to the rural health centre, are considered as providers of primary care, their cost must be separated from the total cost of institutional health care and shown as primary health care investments. To this cost the capital expenditures of urban health facilities clearly providing primary care can be added. Similarly the national capital expenditure on durable equipment, or on water supply, sanitation and nutrition programmes can be apportioned to primary health care. In many countries health buildings are erected using voluntary labour and donated materials. The value of this work should be included.

For many purposes it is useful to bring the costs of water, sanitation and nutrition programmes together. Estimates can be made by aggregating data from local studies.

Classification by source of finance

In view of its importance, care should be taken to identify local informal cooperative insurance arrangements and classify them as private insurance. In a number of countries such systems of insurance have considerable potential for growth.

Examples of tables that can be used for assembling the data are shown in Tables 14 and 15. Similar tables can be used for capital expenditure. For comparisons with past years, the use of a consumer price index is recommended unless a more sophisticated index has been calculated by the central statistics authority.

For further information on primary health care see pages 97, 98, 102, and 103 and Annex 1.

Table 14. Sources of finance for primary
health care over a 4-year period, e.g., 1979–1982 (model)

Source of finance	Constant prices (million NCU[a])				% share			
	1979	1980	1981	1982	1979	1980	1981	1982
Ministry of health								
Other govt. dept.								
Local govt.								
Compulsory health insurance								
Voluntary health insurance								
Private employers								
Local donations (cash)								
Private households								
Donated labour								
External cooperation (official)								
External cooperation (non-official)								
Total					100	100	100	100

[a] NCU = national currency unit.

76

Table 15. Expenditure on primary health care in any one year by source of finance (model)

| Area of expenditure | Public | | | | Private | | | | | External cooperation | |
	Ministry of health	Other govt. dept.	Local govt.	Social insurance	Private health insurance	Private employers	Charity	Donated labour		Official	Non-official
Personal health services											
Health centres											
Health posts											
Private practitioners											
Indigenous health practitioners											
Private dental services											
Communicable disease control											
Health education											
Training											
Health-related activities											
Domestic water supply											
Sanitation											
Nutrition											
Housing											
Total											

CHAPTER 7

Evaluation and the examination of alternatives

Evaluation of the material collected

The collection of all the data showing the present size, distribution and sources of funds used for health is not just an academic exercise. The data provide the necessary factual basis for planning the future size and distribution of expenditures in the health sector and how they will be financed, covering for example:

— the relationship between spending on primary health care and other levels of care;
— the priority to be given to particular programmes within the health services such as malaria or maternal and child health;
— the priority to be given to different techniques of intervention such as immunization, health education and rehabilitation;
— the level of technology to be used in different parts of the health care system;
— the relationship between spending on health services as against health-related activities such as water, sanitation and nutrition;
— the relationship between expenditures on particular age groups;
— the relationship between expenditures per head in different parts of the country, particularly urban and rural areas.

A number of different ways of analysing data for review were set out in Chapter 3 and will not be repeated here. In addition, a set of questions used to analyse health expenditure as part of a teaching programme is shown in Annex 2. The aim of a review is to produce policy options and ultimately decisions on future action. As stated in Chapter 3, the starting-point for a review should be the policy objectives of the particular country as expressed, for example, in the national health plans. Using the data collected it is possible to show in quantitative terms what is currently being spent on particular priorities and the proportion this represents of the total expenditure. In most cases it is on these selected priorities that the country plans to spend more in the future. The extra cost per year of increasing expenditure on these priorities at different rates can now be calculated.

The plan may also define finite longer-term objectives, based on those for the attainment of health for all by the year 2000. They may include:

(*a*) the provision of specific immunizations to all children in a particular age group;

(*b*) the provision of clean water and sanitation to the whole population;

(*c*) access for the total population to primary health care.

Thus the amount currently spent on immunization, on water and sanitation, and on primary health care can be calculated and related to data on coverage. Calculations can then be made of the total capital cost of reaching the long-term objectives and the extra recurrent cost of full coverage. Thus it is possible to calculate how the total capital cost relates to annual current capital expenditure for all health purposes. For example, does the capital requirement represent three times or ten times the annual capital expenditure? Similarly, does the additional recurrent cost require an increase of 5% or 50% of:

(*a*) total public expenditure in the health sector, if financed from public funds;

(*b*) total national expenditure on health and health-related activities, if a variety of sources of finance could be mobilized.

This shows the additional resources that would be required or the cuts that would need to be imposed in lesser priority areas of recurrent expenditure to meet the objective of full coverage. For example, the priority programmes may represent 20% of public expenditure on the health sector but be meeting the needs of only a third of the population. At first sight, therefore, an increase of 40% in total expenditure or a cut of 50% in expenditure on lesser priority programmes would be needed to achieve universal coverage. (In practice, the needs of the uncovered population may cost more or less per head to meet than those of the covered population.)

The review may also contribute to the formation of further objectives or new objectives in the next health plan. Thus the key findings should be summarized at the end of the report with policy options such as the following:

Example 1

The teaching hospital absorbed 20% of public recurrent spending in the health sector and 10% of total health expenditure. Over 90% of the patients (91% of in-patients and 95% of outpatients) came from the capital city where 10% of the population reside.

Policy options

(1) Reduce the cost of the hospital by reducing the staff or transferring beds to other uses.

(2) Improve transport to bring in more patients referred from outside the capital.

(3) Use other hospitals (upgraded) outside the capital for teaching medical students.

Example 2

Expenditure on all hospitals represented 60% of recurrent expenditure in the health sector. Over 85% of patients were drawn from the urban areas, where 24% of the population reside.

Policy options

(1) Reduce the cost of hospital by:

    (*a*) reducing the budget;

    (*b*) reducing staffing;

    (*c*) closing one or more wards as the primary health care system is further developed.

The closing of beds would require more careful selection of patients for admission and/or a reduction in unnecessarily long stays in hospital. Better use of hospitals can also be achieved by preventing duplication where hospitals are operating in local areas under more than one system of ownership.

(2) Introduce charges for certain defined categories of patients.

(3) Improve transport for referred rural patients.

Example 3

Drug expenditure in Region I was twice that in Region II and four times that in Region IV.

Policy options

(1) Introduce charges for drugs in Region I.

(2) Distribute qualified manpower more equitably between the regions.

(3) Check on possible thefts in Region I, and the regular availability of supplies in Region III.

Example 4

In the rural areas, private expenditure on indigenous practitioners was equal to the total recurrent expenditure on curative services provided by the government at all levels, other than in hospitals. The number of consultations with traditional practitioners was twice the number with the government services.

Policy options

(1) Improve training and selection of government health personnel for rural work and improve drug supplies.

(2) Train traditional practitioners and encourage them to work in the government rural services.

(3) Make primary health care more accessible—closer to where the people live.

Example 5

In the rural areas the mission hospitals treat in-patients at half the cost of the government hospitals. Their hospitals have high occupancy rates compared with the low rates of the government hospitals.

Policy options

(1) Consult the local people on why they under-use government hospitals.

(2) Review the efficiency and administrative practices of government hospitals.

(3) Invite the mission hospitals to take over the running of low occupancy government hospitals with a government subsidy.

(4) Close low occupancy government hospitals and subsidize an expansion in mission hospitals.

Planning for the extra resources required
for the growth of priority programmes

Extra resources for priority programmes can be found in three ways:

(1) by improving the efficiency of the existing services and of the operation of the financing mechanism;

(2) by introducing more appropriate technology in the more costly services;

(3) by mobilizing new sources of funds.

The report should examine the possibilities in each of these options and present the alternatives and their consequences for political decision. Inevitably, the decisions are highly political. Options which are acceptable in one country may well be unacceptable in another. Moreover, there cannot be gainers without there also being losers. And this is true not only in terms of who bears the cost, but also in terms of professional opportunities for particular types of practice.

Improving the efficiency of existing services and of the operation of the financing mechanism

The most painless way of finding resources for the growth of priority services is by improving efficiency—for example, better control of supplies to cut down waste and pilferage or more skilled purchasing of drugs. Efficiency can also be improved by reducing the number of vacant beds in hospitals and cutting down on unnecessarily long lengths of stay. The aim should be to manage with fewer beds and close whole wards or whole hospitals or transfer services to parts of the country where services are overstretched. Such policies can be pursued at the same time as primary health care services are improved and extended to provide alternative patterns of care in the community. In some specific fields, for example, in immunization and water supply programmes, cost-effectiveness studies can usefully be applied.

Control action should aim to influence the behaviour of both providers and users. One means of influencing user behaviour is by introducing, increasing or extending charges for certain types of health care, an option which is discussed later in this chapter.

The unit costs of providing particular services in different hospitals, health centres, etc., can be compared and ways found to improve efficiency where unit costs are unjustifiably high. In some cases it may be more efficient to subsidize missions and employers to provide certain services for the whole local population than it wound be to provide competing services run by government. Similarly, the subsidizing of services run by local community groups (e.g., agricultural cooperatives) may be more efficient and secure greater local participation than services provided by government. In some countries social security, charity and government hospitals duplicate each others' services in local areas. Economies can be secured by the rationalization of function and by enabling all categories of user to be treated in the same establishment so that one or more hospitals can be closed or diverted to other uses inside or outside the health sector.

In some countries, excessive rates of pay or overgenerous terms of service (e.g., short hours) are given to particular grades of professional staff because of competition between sectors (social security, government, industry or missions). This problem could be overcome by standardizing either the terms of service in each sector or the establishments for the various units in each sector, for the particular grade of scarce manpower.

Similar pressure may come from competition from the private sector. This can be of special importance where rewards in the private sector are such that trained persons are unwilling to accept appointments in the organized health services, particularly for work in rural areas. One option is to institute charges for licences to engage in private practice in particular geographical areas. Another is to levy taxes on private health care expenditures.

Identifying and analysing the channels through which monetary resources flow and gathering information on the practical operation of the public and private financing system may lead to conclusions related to the financial management of the health sector. For example, the study may show that programmed and budgeted funds do not actually reach certain services or certain levels of services in time, because budgetary decision-making is overcentralized and the release of funds is linked with the *de facto* receipt of revenues by the ministry of finance. This may be extremely harmful for the running of particular services: purchase orders for supplies may not be cleared, suppliers may charge higher prices (adding interest on payments made after considerable delay), shortages in medicaments may seriously interfere with the functioning of health units. To diagnose and be denied the supplies needed to treat is a near-total waste of resources. While national financial systems are difficult to change, improvements—for example, by the decentralization of budgetary control—may be recommended. Similarly, measures for improving accounting and financial practices in different parts of the health system may be proposed.

Introducing more appropriate technology

The aim should be to find lower-cost technologies which are no less effective. As care in hospital is expensive, admission should be avoided whenever possible and cheaper alternatives developed. Patients with leprosy or tuberculosis can be satisfactorily treated, and a very large amount of mental illness handled, in the community. Oral rehydration can also prevent admission to hospital. Many elementary surgical procedures can be performed on a day basis when adequate post-operative nursing can be provided.

Complex mechanical equipment is often imported by developing countries (at a high cost in foreign exchange) which is frequently out of order because it is awaiting either repair or the import of spare parts. It may also be subject to frequent and dangerous stoppages if the local electrical supply is overloaded or unreliable. Less sophisticated equipment may give a more reliable service to more patients and be more cost-effective. Similarly, natural ventilation may be less comfortable than air-conditioning but at least it never breaks down. Ramps may be a laborious way of transporting patients and supplies between levels of a hospital but unlike lifts they are unlikely to break down.

Economies can be made in the purchase of supplies by the use of local materials whenever these would be cheaper; for example, the perfect finish of factory-made furniture can be dispensed with and small sterilizers can readily be improvised. A drug list used in primary health care can be reduced to what is really essential, and greater skill in tendering can gain the lowest prices for products shown by test to be of the designated quality. Local processing of some drugs can be encouraged when it would be cheaper in the long run.

Tasks should be delegated to the lowest level of staff that can be trained to perform them effectively. There is a strong case for every highly trained grade to be matched by a corresponding auxiliary grade to whom tasks can be delegated. This is true not only of physicians but of dentists, pharmacists, health inspectors, nurses, sanitary engineers, and many others. Auxiliaries can be trained quicker than full professionals and thus can be in the field sooner than more highly trained staff.

Thus costs can be saved, particularly in in-patient care, by a concerted plan to move to a lower level of technology. Control can be exercised by the regulation of establishment or by reducing budgets (or not increasing them in line with rising costs). The construction of new hospitals outside the public sector can be regulated by refusing licences for construction or by regulating the use of qualified manpower. In general, cost containment measures must always take account of their likely effect on the quality of care. Financial containment measures should therefore be combined with measures to influence the pattern of health care delivery.

Mobilizing additional funds

Taxes

It is often argued that some new tax should be levied to finance an expanded health programme. It is not, however, always the case that such a tax will advance the cause of health. It all depends on whom the burden of the tax ultimately falls. While income tax is progressive, most indirect taxes fall most heavily on the poor. Making the poor poorer by taxation could do more harm than good as regards health. It is often argued that the revenue from taxes on products such as tobacco or alcohol should be used exclusively for health purposes. Ministries of finance are, however, generally reluctant to earmark taxes for particular purposes. And if they are finally persuaded to do so, they are likely to argue that funds made available from other taxes should be cut by precisely the estimated revenue of the ear-marked tax. Thus departments responsible for health and health-related expenditures may be no better off.

Moreover, they may be tied to taxes whose revenue declines each year. In so far as higher taxes may reduce productive investment, the improvement in health through higher living standards may be postponed.

Compulsory health insurance

The introduction of a compulsory health insurance scheme is clearly one way of raising additional revenue, though, again, ministries of finance may argue that direct and indirect taxes should be cut by an equivalent amount.

Those who favour compulsory health insurance argue that:

(*a*) it brings extra funds to the health sector and channels them into organized health services: these funds cannot be used for any purpose other than health;

(*b*) workers protected by compulsory health insurance do not have to pay the high fees charged in private practice, since the charges for services are determined by negotiation between the insurance agency and the health care providers;

(*c*) compulsory health insurance creates incentives for the construction of hospitals in the private sector and the training of health manpower—this will relieve the burden on public health services so that they can devote more resources to the uninsured;

(*d*) experience has shown that both legislative and executive branches of government are usually more favourable to the development of compulsory health insurances than to significant increases in general revenue funds allotted for health purposes.

The objections most often raised to compulsory insurance systems are:

(1) as workers who can pay contributions tend to be concentrated in cities and towns, the maldistribution of resources between urban and rural areas is likely to be aggravated;

(2) the relatively few persons who are already privileged by having regular cash earnings would benefit from a subsidized health care system; the sources of subsidy are taxes disguised as compulsory insurance contributions which should be used to contribute to the health care of the most underprivileged categories of the population;

(3) the health policies developed by ministries of health may have only limited influence on compulsory health insurance systems, which are usually heavily oriented towards curative services;

(4) the existence of compulsory health insurance may make it even more difficult to recruit personnel for public health services which are attempting to serve the whole population;

(5) compulsory health insurance involves a costly administrative structure which has to be paid for by the funds raised, and thus uses considerable resources for purposes other than health.

Countries contemplating the introduction of compulsory health insurance schemes need to consider in advance how and when such a programme can be implemented. It should not be introduced until the trained manpower is available, not only to work in the programme but also to meet all planned extensions without reducing other existing services. If social security is extended to rural areas, it will be necessary to develop financial and service delivery mechanisms that are suited to the characteristics of the population to be protected (for further details on social security see reference *19*).

In nearly all cases, compulsory health insurance has been developed in countries where: (*a*) there was no shortage of medical manpower by the standards then prevailing; and (*b*) the only services available free were low-standard services provided by charity or poor law legislation for the indigent. Compulsory health insurance was thus a way of financing a right to better, or at least more acceptable, services for those with a regular job.

In some developing countries free services are already available and accessible at least to the urban population. Workers and employers will not willingly contribute to compulsory health insurance unless contributors (and their dependents) obtain something distinctly better in return for the contributions. In countries with a shortage of doctors and dentists, little more can be provided than higher standards of amenity in hospital without drawing away trained manpower from the services provided for those from whom contributions cannot be collected. Thus the price paid for better services for those who can pay will be worse services for those who cannot.

If contributors come to regard compulsory health insurance contributions simply as taxes, they and their employers may try to avoid payment, and a continuous and far from successful battle will be fought to secure compliance.

Thus in some countries the state of existing services and particularly the availability and likelihood of recruiting trained manpower can make compulsory health insurance an unviable option. In others, the option may be practicable.

Voluntary health insurance schemes

Insurance schemes can undoubtedly contribute to the financing of health care. However, if major schemes are developed, legislation and financial regulations may be needed to protect the interests of the public sector. For example, where public and private insurance systems are operating simultaneously, private insurance schemes may attempt to attract low-risk persons and exclude those with high risks, leaving them to be covered by the public scheme. In consequence, the public schemes may require subsidies from public funds, while the private schemes

88

make profits. Moreover, the introduction of private insurance can, as in the case of compulsory insurance, make excessive demands on scarce manpower and make it more difficult to recruit trained personnel to work in government services, particularly in rural areas. On the other hand, schemes limited to a relatively small section of the more affluent who already use private practitioners may relieve the load on "pay beds" provided in government hospitals by encouraging the use of private hospitals. But this may not actually save money in government hospitals; beds which are not used by those who are insured may be rapidly filled up by those who are not and pay nothing for using them. The introduction of formal voluntary insurance schemes should be preceded by studies analysing all these relevant implications.

To examine the potential role of private health insurance and the effects of alternative types of development, data should be collected on such schemes as exist. These can be assembled partly by contacting major employers and/or trade unions which have schemes (many such employers are likely to be known by the ministry of labour) and partly by contacting the major insurers. While some schemes may operate through insurance companies, others may operate through a welfare fund set up by the particular employer or trade union. Data need to be collected on the number of persons covered, the rates of contribution and, where relevant, how they are split between employers and employees, the range of benefits provided, and any monetary or other limits or cost-sharing. An indication is also needed of the income level of the insured persons.

Parallel to this, information can be collected from certain key providers. For example, managers of nursing homes and private hospitals and those collecting charges for pay-beds in government hospitals can be asked what proportion of their receipts come from, or on behalf of, persons who are insured.

Once estimates have been made of the current role of private insurance, the potential for expansion can be examined. How many additional employees and individual contributors might be covered, taking into account the size and prosperity of particular fields of employment and the distribution of income among individuals? Health insurance could be promoted by aggressive salesmanship directed either at employers or individual contributors. Alternatively, employers in particular industries could be required to pay for health services (by insurance or otherwise) for all their employees or, at least, their better paid employees. What proportionate expansion of the private sector would be required to meet this potential demand? Could this be accommodated without drawing scarce trained manpower (such as doctors, nurses and dentists) out of the government services and making it more difficult to staff the rural areas?

Clearly desirable are less formal systems of community funding of primary health care. The following examples drawn from the experience of developing countries could be more widely applied:

— the villagers establish and operate village pharmacies; the initial stock of medicaments is bought at harvest time and replenished from user payments;

— rural maternity centres, serving a group of villages, are built by villagers, who donate labour and local materials; the services are provided by rotational teams of traditional birth attendants; small fees are collected from users to cover recurrent costs;

— citizens' committees are created to support village health workers, health posts, and rural health centres; modest fees from users of services finance the salaries of health personnel and the purchase of drugs;

— the system of rural water supply is built by the donated labour of villagers; recurrent costs are financed by users' fees;

— teams of health providers create local, "grass roots" health insurance; for modest contributions families are entitled to medical care provided at clinics;

— farmers produce medical herbs from seeds provided by the authorities; these herbs are purchased and distributed through the official health services.

Charging-out costs to those who generate them

The costs of road accidents falling on health services can be charged to those who own motorized vehicles. To do this in each individual case would be an extremely complex administrative operation, involving vehicle owners, their insurers and the health services. Moreover, it would be argued that health service costs should only be paid by or on behalf of the owner of a vehicle who was at fault in causing them. This would introduce further legal and administrative complexities. The simplest solution, where it is acceptable, is a requirement for vehicle owners to insure against this risk for drivers, passengers and others and a surcharge on all insurance policies to be distributed among the providers of health care.

90

Similarly, employers can be required to insure against the risk of health service costs arising out of injuries at work. Again, the collection of the revenue from insurance companies as a lump sum per employee insured saves administrative costs for all concerned and makes the proposition much more viable.

For obvious reason these options are easiest to apply where a government health service provides care to the vast majority of such cases.

Charges to users of services

Paying directly for services, including health care, is a long-established way of financing health activities. It is found in all countries, particularly for the services of traditional practitioners. The arguments for and against "free" services in the public sector are continuously debated. Advocates of free public health services argue that:

(1) each citizen is entitled to a minimal level of health services;

(2) introduction of even modest fees would hit the poorest, who are often the neediest;

(3) collection, accounting, and administration of fees create costly bureaucratic problems and any system devised to try to exempt the poor will be "rough justice".

Advocates of charges maintain that:

(a) fees add to the finance of services and thus improve them;

(b) people value more highly services for which they pay and thus a more cost-conscious atmosphere is created;

(c) certificates to exempt the poor and other methods (e.g., a fee system following the geographical income pattern of the country) could satisfy the requirements of social justice;

(d) even small fees will reduce the unnecessary use of services and particularly the consumption of medicaments, and thus help cost-containment.

In the private sector the fee system has to be seen both from the point of view of the public (affordable, accessible) and the point of view of the providers. The interrelationships between the public and private sectors' fee systems have also to be considered in terms of the availability of personnel, quality of services, etc. Studies analysing the issues involved are essential and will need to take into account the overall economic situation of the country.

Charges or fees can be used to secure greater equity between urban and rural services. Where, as is often the case, urban services are much more highly staffed, those who use them can be charged, while no charges are made for the use of the simpler rural services. The revenue can be used to help finance improvements in rural services.

Charges or fees can be used to back up systems of referral between primary health care and secondary care. In many developing countries, the habit has become established for people to flock to the outpatient departments of the main hospitals for minor health problems, bypassing their local system of primary health care on the way. Substantial charges can be levied on persons visiting outpatient departments who have not been referred except in clear cases of accident or emergency. Those who are referred from primary health care can be exempted from the charge.

In some countries, private rooms in government hospitals ("pay-beds") are provided at substantially less than the cost this service entails. Such rooms may be used by the more affluent section of the population, thus undercutting private hospitals. They may also be used by foreign visitors, including tourists. In some cases these rooms may be provided without charge to certain categories of user. Charging the full cost of the service to all users is one way of increasing the revenue earned by the public sector. If certain specialized units are available only in government hospitals, these units should incorporate pay-beds for which full cost is charged. There is no reason to force better-off patients to receive services free, and with a lower standard of amenity, that they would willingly buy from the private sector if they were available.

The revenue from charges can be calculated as follows:

(1) The revenue is estimated on the assumption that no one is exempted and the whole potential revenue is actually collected. For example, the potential yield of a flat-rate charge per day in hospital can be calculated as the rate of charge multiplied by the number of hospital days provided. A charge per outpatient visit can be calculated similarly from data on the number of such visits.

(2) Revenue not collected from persons exempt from the charge is deducted. Exemptions may be required for medical reasons (e.g., infectious diseases), for social reasons (e.g., the elderly, children, the poor), or for reasons of public policy (e.g., health personnel, policemen injured on duty).

(3) Allowance is made for any reduction in usage by those still subject to the charge.

(4) Allowance is made for bad debts and other failures in the collection system.

(5) Allowance is made for the administrative costs of collection. When exemptions are complex, these costs can be considerable.

External cooperation

Recommendations may indicate the share of the total costs and the type of services or activities proposed for funding from external sources. Discrepancies between the magnitude and pattern of the present flow of external cooperation (technical advice, supplies, research, financial transfers) and the requirements of the primary health care plan can be pointed out. Methods for better national coordination of external resources may be proposed. Attention may also be drawn to special obstacles to external funding.

Countries need specialized staff to maximize income from potential foreign donors. Such staff ascertain the types of project likely to interest particular donors, draft applications, and arrange systems of evaluation when these are required. However, some gifts may, through capital expenditure, generate recurrent expenditure that is of very low priority in terms of national priorities. The aim of policy is to maximize external aid that fits in with planned developments. There are some gifts countries cannot afford to accept.

Conclusion

It is not enough to conclude a study with a series of tables and leave them to speak for themselves. A country which has prepared a health plan intends to implement it. A way has to be found to finance the programmes selected for development. There are only two ways of doing this. Either money has to be found from savings in programmes of lesser priority, or new money has to be raised to finance the developments—either from home sources or from foreign sources. The data collected in the study should be used to quantify the cost of developments in the planned directions at different rates and set out all possible options for finding the money for expenditures arising from political decisions.

CHAPTER 8

Projections of future expenditure and sources of finance

In the past, the health plans of ministries of health normally covered only the public sector, and often did not include intersectoral activities. Health plans were traditionally prepared in "physical terms", covering such items as manpower, facilities and supplies, and the running costs of health institutions. To aid communication between the ministry of finance and the ministry of health the plans followed the same general lines as were used in the government accounts. Often they were built up from "shopping lists" prepared by those responsible for particular parts of the services. Inevitably each head of department could readily find areas of pressure that could be relieved or services of higher technology that could be introduced. If new buildings (e.g., a new hospital) were due to come into service during the planning period, these would be shown as a further demand for funds on top of other demands. The costs of the planned activities and programmes were estimated and then compared with the amount of funding that could reasonably be expected. The plan was then revised (usually reduced) in accordance with policy and other priorities according to the level of funding negotiated with the ministry of finance. The latter would be likely to argue that there should be economies elsewhere if a new hospital was due to be opened and cut the budget requested on this assumption. After all the cuts, the balance of the original plan, i.e., new posts, equipment or units of lesser priority remained a complement to the plan—to be implemented only if funds became available later on.

The principles of this method were usually also observed during the implementation of the plan. If programmed and budgeted funds were reduced by central authorities or other sources of funds (e.g., the ministry of finance or a foreign donor), unavoidable commitments, such as payment of salaries of health personnel, were honoured. In other areas (e.g., purchase of drugs) expenditures were reduced, initially

95

by running down stocks, and even to the extent of supplies running out before the end of the financial year.

Because of the unsatisfactory consequences of this method of proceeding, the following new approaches are recommended:

(1) Public health planners and administrators plan for the whole health sector, including other government departments, local government, compulsory health insurance, voluntary bodies, industry, and the whole private sector.

(2) As mentioned in Chapter 7, estimates are made of the total cost of achieving particular finite objectives such as a system of primary health care accessible to the whole population, or clean water and sanitation made available to all. A proportion of the cost is then put into the planning period making it clear that the aim is to complete the whole programme by, for example, the year 1990 or 2000.

(3) Capital expenditure (both new buildings and additions to buildings) and training are planned as a consequence of longer-term plans for recurrent expenditure rather than separately. It is increasingly recognized that the process of building or training personnel in the hope that ministries of finance will find extra funds over and above other priorities to avoid such embarrassments as "mothballed" (i.e., unopened) hospitals or unemployed physicians trained at public expense, has in the past led to the distortion of planned priorities. When ministries of finance were unable to find the funds for both types of development, other higher priorities for development had to be cut to find the money to pay for the running costs of new hospitals and to employ newly trained physicians. To avoid this:

— *estimates of recurrent cost need to be made before any capital expenditure is undertaken, the estimates being built into the plan; and*

— *the cost of employing staff needs to be estimated and built into the plan before training is undertaken.*

(4) Sources of finance to pay for the whole health sector are identified, including financing by communities in the form of cooperative insurance or private payments. This plan for financing has to be realistic and wholly compatible with the plan for health care and health-related activities.

Thus the starting-point for projections of future expenditure is a clear statement of objectives. The analysis of expenditure and sources of finance may have contributed to a reformulation of these objectives. National objectives may be considered separately from local objectives, or local objectives may be incorporated in national objectives. Many of these objectives may be long-term in the sense that it would not be practicable to realize them fully in a medium-term plan covering five years because, for example, of the need to train further personnel or new categories of personnel.

In countries which adopt the primary health care approach in total, primary health care gradually replaces all vertical programmes. There are in effect two *main* operational programmes—primary health care and the specialist and hospital services (the secondary and tertiary services) to which referrals are made from primary care. Developments in these two programmes compete for financial resources and yet are completementary. But the crucial point is that the potential sources of finance for the two programmes may be very different.

Primary health care

The questions raised in the design of a programme of primary health care to cover the whole nation are fundamental. Primary health care is intended to meet basic health needs. How should these needs be defined, how should they be met, and who should make these decisions? In the past, providers of health care have played a decisive role in making these decisions. Recently, other professionals with training in promoting the general process of development have had a say. But the primary health care approach as approved by the World Health Assembly strongly emphasizes the right both of local communities and of individuals to decide about their health needs and how they should be met in the same way as they should decide about other basic human needs. Under this approach, programmes developed locally need to be costed and aggregated on a national basis.

The first step is to make an estimate of the total recurrent cost of a chosen system of primary health care that is accessible to all and makes use of an appropriate level of technology. This can be compared with expenditure calculated as in Chapter 6 for the existing primary care provisions. The difference between these two figures represents the additional financial resources to be found—though not all of this is likely to be achievable in a five-year period.

The ultimate pattern of primary health care chosen will have implications for capital expenditure. New buildings will have to be built and some existing buildings will need to be upgraded. The total capital programme needs to be estimated, even though a considerable part of the cost may ultimately be found from donated labour and materials. The programme will also have implications for training. The total cost of training all the extra personnel and retraining existing personnel needs to be calculated.

The rate of progress towards the full programme may be limited by the rate at which the training can be completed and the capital expenditure undertaken, more than by the availability of resources. What is important, however, is that capital expenditure and expenditure on training are geared to the projected growth of recurrent expenditure on primary health care.

Secondary and tertiary services

The approach to the secondary and tertiary sectors should be similar except for one crucial difference. Major capital works may already be in progress or a gift of a hospital from an external donor may have been accepted. The recurrent cost of these developments should be calculated and shown provisionally as additional costs for the years from which the new facilities are expected to become operational.

Estimates need to be made of the recurrent costs of the total secondary and tertiary services needed to support the fully developed primary programme. These recurrent costs will require further capital expenditure and further expenditure on training which also need to be geared to the projected growth of recurrent expenditure. The extra recurrent cost of fully developed secondary and tertiary services over existing secondary and tertiary services can then be calculated. Part of these costs will be already included in the recurrent cost of present capital schemes mentioned in the previous paragraph.

Inevitably there will be demands coming from within the existing secondary and tertiary services for extra expenditure to relieve pressures on staff, to buy additional equipment and to develop new units. The costs of all these internally generated demands should be aggregated, whether they come from government, compulsory health insurance, mission or other services. Only when all demands are put alongside each other—those which are being currently articulated from within the service, those which will be articulated when new capital facilities are completed, and those which will emerge in the future as the primary health care programme spreads and extends access, which

98

is in turn likely to have implications for secondary and tertiary services—only then can choices be made on expenditure projected for the next five years.

If estimates are not made of future expenditure not currently being articulated, demands which are being articulated are likely to be met *solely for this reason*. Those with no services, negligible services, or exclusively traditional services tend often to be the silent majority. Their requirements are crowded out by the continuous preemption of resources in giving more to those best served at present, often with a level of technology that cannot be financed for all. The priorities enunciated in national plans for development and the priorities in the spending of extra money can end up in near-total contradiction.

The presentation of options

All the options should be worked out in some detail, as indicated below. Separate calculations should be made for primary health care and for the secondary and tertiary services.

Investments

In planning these, it is important to include the cost of construction and the operational cost to be incurred, once the health facility is functioning, by level of planned health facilities (primary, secondary, tertiary) and their geographical location. Where possible, information on the expected costs (fixed and variable) of health institutions should be assembled.

Recurrent costs

The following items require consideration:

Manpower training plans—different categories of health personnel, number of trainees, cost of training per category, expected area of activity, (e.g., institutional care or individual practice).

Manpower deployment plans—geographical deployment of the newly trained personnel (including estimates for the private sector),

99

estimated salaries or income per category of personnel (personnel for insitutional health care, ambulatory care, or other types of service).

Costs of public health services—supplies (showing medicaments separately) and equipment, maintenance of buildings and equipment (by geographical area and by level of care, i.e., primary, secondary), other costs (i.e., subsidies, cost of administration).

Cost of private health services—cost of private hospitals; amounts spent on private practitioners (from public funds and in private payments), including traditional healers; cost of medicaments.

Cost of water supply, sanitation and nutritional programmes

Projections can be obtained from the same sources as data on past expenditure and financing.

The choice of what to include in the immediate planning period can only proceed by trial and error. In the case of the private sector, a starting-point may be the forward projection of past trends at rates identified over recent years. It will normally fall to the organized sector to reflect national priorities. The priorities that have been laid down must be seen to be observed in any projections of costs. The plan must show a noticeable shift in the proportion of resources going into these priority areas. More than one sector of finance may contribute to this shift—not only government but compulsory health insurance, industry, missions and external aid. The problem is to decide on the quantity of the shift in each priority direction to occur within the next five-year planning period. This will depend in part on political decisions about savings elsewhere or new sources of finance made on the basis of the options presented in the last chapter. But any switch in resources will have to be compatible with new facilities completed, the timing of new capital projects, the output of trained manpower, and the ability of planners to secure that newly qualified manpower do work where their services are most needed. Above all else, a plan for projected costs must be capable of being financed by the sources of finance selected. Each draft of projected costs must be tested against these criteria until options are found which:

(1) show a noticeable shift towards each priority objective;

(2) allow for all or part of new capital facilities currently being constructed to be brought into use;

100

(3) provide for further new capital projects to be completed in time to be used during the planning period and later planning periods;

(4) are compatible with expenditure on training and the output of trained personnel for this planning period and for later planning periods;

(5) can be paid for by identified sources of finance which are politically acceptable.

Tables showing projections of costs for the viable options should be expressed in constant prices and can follow the same format as Tables 1, 2, 11, and 12 but covering the next five years. Similarly, tables for primary health care should follow the format of Tables 3, 13, and 14. The viable options may differ principally in the rate at which deserved objectives are achieved.

Conclusion

The generation of new funds and the improved distribution of available funds are central concerns of the health planning process. The policy of health for all by the year 2000 is to provide health care for those not at present covered. In many developing countries, the public sector is unlikely to obtain sufficient additional funds to expand health services in their present form. Thus there is a need to change the proportion of different categories of manpower, to use appropriate (i.e., affordable) health care technologies, to mobilize new resources, and to prepare projections for the whole health sector.

Where particular budgets (e.g., ministry of health) are expected to be limited, imaginative plans for reallocations will need to be made. Cost projections must be in line with the level of funds expected from the ministry of finance. The ministry of health may need to make fewer demands for funds if by doing so the ministry of finance is enabled to make more funds available for health-related activities that are financed by other government departments and judged to be of higher priority. If new funds cannot be obtained (e.g., from external cooperation), the financial provision for some services may need to be cut to make room for new developments, or costs may need to be shifted on to other sources of finance by, for example, introducing charges for particular services or raising charges for particular users (e.g., private wards). Original estimates for the recurrent costs of using new facilities may need to be reduced by using less manpower, lesser trained manpower and less sophisticated equipment. Or the use of a new facility may need to be phased in over a number of years. Those demanding more may have to be given less and ways found of reducing their workload by establishing a clearer system of priorities. Only thus may those currently denied access to services be given effective access to them.

The task is to produce projections of cost which are viable and meet all the criteria listed above. The ultimate test of viability is success in implementation. Thus subsequent studies of expenditure and sources of finance can be used to identify what went wrong with the earlier projections—to evaluate past experience and use the information

Table 16. Projections of expenditure for primary health care
over a 4-year period, e.g., 1982–1985 (model)

Area of expenditure	Projected expenditure (million NCU[a])				% change		
	1982	1983	1984	1985	1983	1984	1985
Health							
Health centres							
Health posts							
Private practitioners							
Indigenous health practitioners							
Private dental services							
Communicable disease control							
Health education							
Training							
Health-related activities							
Domestic water supply							
Sanitation							
Nutrition							
Housing							
Total							

[a] NCU = national currency unit.

102

obtained to improve the next series of projections. That is why it was stressed in earlier chapters that studies of this kind should be repeated periodically so that plans are rolling plans backed up by realistic financial assessments.

This chapter has set out to show how a "master plan for the use of all financial and material resources" (see page 13) can be developed and used as an integral part of the planning process and thus assist developing countries in achieving their health objectives. This is the ultimate test of whether it is worth the effort to undertake studies of this kind.

Tables 16 and 17 illustrate how financial projections can be organized. Similar tables can be used for projecting future capital expenditures.

Table 17. Projections of funding for health
by sources of finance over a 4-year period, e.g., 1982–1985 (model)[a]

Source of finance	Projected expenditure (million NCU[b])				% share			
	1982	1983	1984	1985	1982	1983	1984	1985
Total health expenditure								
Government								
Social insurance								
Private employers								
Private households								
External cooperation (official)								
External cooperation (non-official)								
Total					100	100	100	100
Total expenditure on primary health care								
Government								
Social insurance								
Private employers								
Private householders								
External cooperation (official)								
External cooperation (non-official)								
Total					100	100	100	100

[a] A similar table can be devised for future capital expenditure.
[b] NCU = national currency unit.

REFERENCES AND FURTHER READING

1. ABEL-SMITH, B. *An international study of health expenditure, and its relevance for health planning.* Geneva, World Health Organization, 1967 (Public Health Papers, No. 32).

2. ABEL-SMITH, B. *Poverty, development and health policy.* Geneva, World Health Organization, 1978 (Public Health Papers, No. 69).

3. AMERICAN PUBLIC HEALTH ASSOCIATION. *Health care financing in Central America and the Andean region:* Report of a workshop, Melgar, Colombia, 23-27 April 1979, Washington, DC, 1979.

4. COMMONWEALTH DEPARTMENT OF HEALTH. *Australian health expenditure 1974–75 to 1977–78: an analysis.* Canberra, Australian Government Publishing Service, 1980.

5. DEEBLE, J.S. & SCOTT, I.W. *Health expenditure in Australia 1960–61 to 1975–76.* Australian National University, Canberra, 1978 (Australian National University Research Project: Research Report No. 1).

6. DEPARTMENT OF HEALTH & AUSTRALIAN BUREAU OF STATISTICS assisted by W.D. SCOTT & CO. PTY. LTD. *National Health account—a study.* Canberra, Australian Government Publishing Service, 1978.

7. DJUKANOVIC, V. & MACH, E.P., ED. *Alternative approaches to meeting basic health needs in developing countries.* Geneva, World Health Organization, 1975.

8. GRIFFITH, D.A.T. & MILLS, M.H. *Money for health; a manual for surveys in developing countries.* Geneva, Sandoz Institute for Health and Socio-Economic Studies and the Republic of Botswana (Sandoz Institute, Third World Series, No. 3) (in press).

9. KAM, M.P. *Methodology for the survey and analysis of health financing and expenditure in Botswana,* Botswana Ministry of Health, 1978.

10. LAURENT, A. *Le financement des services de santé au Rwanda.* Geneva, Sandoz Institute for Health and Socio-Economic Studies, 1978.

11. MACH, E.P. The financing of health systems in developing countries. *Social science and medicine,* **12**: 7–11 (1978).

12. MACH, E.P. From health policy to economic action—financing a suitable tool to adapt health programmes to national priorities. *Médecine sociale et préventive,* **24**(2–3): 132–136 (1979).

13. MARTINS, J.M. *The financing of health services in Australia.* Sydney, Health Commission of New South Wales, 1975.

14. MINISTRY OF HEALTH, BOTSWANA. *Financing of health services in Botswana,* Botswana, 1977.

15. MINISTRY OF HEALTH, BOTSWANA. *The financing of health services and activities in Botswana. Second study—1979.* Botswana, 1979.

16. MINISTRY OF HEALTH, COLOMBIA. *Gasto institucional en salud, 1977.* Bogotá, Office of Planning, Finance Division, Ministry of Health, 1980.

17. NATIONAL HEALTH PLANNING UNIT, MINISTRY OF HEALTH, GHANA. *Financial planning and budgeting for the delivery of health services. Manual No. 3.* Accra, Ministry of Health, 1979.

18. ROBERTSON, L., ZSCHOCK, D.K. & DALY, J.A. *Guidelines for analysis of health sector financing in developing countries,* Rockville, MD, USDHEW, Office of International Health, 1979 (International Health Planning Methods Series, No. 8; DHEW Publication No. (PHS) 79–50087).

19. WHO Technical Report Series, No. 625, 1978.

20. WORLD HEALTH ORGANIZATION. *Development of indicators for monitoring progress towards health for all by the year 2000.* Geneva, 1981 ("Health for All" Series No. 4).

21. WORLD HEALTH ORGANIZATION. *Formulating strategies for health for all by the year 2000. Guiding principles and essential issues.* Geneva, 1979 ("Health for All" Series No. 2).

22. WORLD HEALTH ORGANIZATION. *Global strategy for health for all by the year 2000.* Geneva, 1981 ("Health for All" Series No. 3).

23. WORLD HEALTH ORGANIZATION. *Handbook of resolutions and decisions of the World Health Assembly and the Executive Board,* Volume I, Geneva (resolutions EB11.R57.6 and WHA6.27).

24. WORLD HEALTH ORGANIZATION. *Health programme evaluation. Guiding principles.* Geneva, 1981 ("Health for All" Series No. 6).

25. WORLD HEALTH ORGANIZATION. *Managerial process for national health development. Guiding principles.* Geneva, 1981 ("Health for All" Series No. 5).

26. WORLD HEALTH ORGANIZATION. *Plan of action for implementing the global strategy for health for all.* Geneva, 1982 ("Health for All" Series No. 7).

27. WORLD HEALTH ORGANIZATION. *Primary health care. Report of the International Conference on Primary Health Care, Alma-Ata...,* Geneva, 1978 ("Health for All" Series No. 1).

28. WORLD HEALTH ORGANIZATION. *Seventh general programme of work covering the period 1984–1989.* Geneva, 1982 ("Health for All" Series No. 8).

29. WORLD HEALTH ORGANIZATION, REGIONAL OFFICE FOR EUROPE. *Guidelines for health care practice in relation to cost-effectiveness: report on a WHO Workshop.* Copenhagen, 1981 (EURO Reports and Studies, No. 53).

30. WORLD HEALTH ORGANIZATION, REGIONAL OFFICE FOR EUROPE. *Control of health care costs in social security systems: report on a Workshop.* Copenhagen, 1982 (EURO Reports and Studies, No. 55).

Annex 1

EXAMPLES OF COMPLETED TABLES

The data in Table 1A (page 111) show estimated national recurrent expenditure and sources of financing for 1980/1981 and are based on a case study undertaken in a developing country. They show the following main points:

— 60.2% of the ministry of health budget is spent on hospitals;

— 34.4% of the ministry of health budget is spent on the two central hospitals and one general hospital;

— the ministry pays for the training of "other" health staff, not for doctors or dentists;

— the ministry provides a subsidy of 1 115 000 national currency units to the mission hospitals;

— headquarters administration represents 16.1% of the ministry's budget.

The information would be more meaningful if data were available for several past years thus showing trends.

Recurrent expenditures

Further analysis of Table 1A shows that only 39.4% of the total health sector expenditure is financed by the ministry of health. The second largest source is direct private payments (31.8%). The third largest contributors are official and private foreign aid (12.4%). Other ministries and local government pay 8.8% of the sector's total recurrent expenditure. The amount shown in the "insurance" column against "other services" should probably be shown as payment for hospital services and payment to other health care providers; however, the breakdown of the sum was not available, when this particular case study was carried out.

The total amount spent is roughly divided as follows:
— 30% on health care in hospitals;
— 10% on care in other health facilities;
— 7% on care by private practitioners and traditional healers;
— 8.5% on drugs and supplies;
— 5% on special health programmes (communicable diseases control);
— 23.1% on other health-related programmes (domestic water supply, sanitation, nutritional programmes);
— 16.4% on training, management, transport, etc.

The tables prepared so far do not show either the geographical distribution of the health facilities, or the urban/rural breakdown of users. This is an important area for further work.

Table 1A indicates that the ministry of health spends its funds mainly on hospitals, a number of specialized health programmes, headquarters administration and training of staff other than physicians and dentists, and provides a considerable subsidy for mission hospitals.

Other ministries and local government spend modest amounts on hospitals, but their contribution to communicable disease control, domestic water supply, sanitation and nutrition programmes and transport is substantial. *Local government* in particular takes care of the financing of dispensaries and maternity centres, a part of the sanitation and nutrition programme, and the cost of its own administration.

Expenditures incurred by *missions and industry* are spent on curative services.

Data in the *direct private payments* column show that the population contributes to the cost of hospitals, and spends considerable amounts on drugs (22.9% of all direct private payments) and domestic water supplies (40.3% of all direct private payments). An important finding is that about 22% of private payments are made to private health practitioners and traditional healers.

The share of foreign aid in the total recurrent sector expenditure is relatively high, mainly because of the considerable amount spent on nutrition programmes. Training programmes and assistance to communicable disease control are also major items under official foreign aid. Private foreign aid is mainly used to finance running costs of health facilities, provide drug supplies and contribute to the cost of controlling communicable diseases.

Expenditure on primary health care

Estimates of the cost of primary health care are shown in Table 2A, assuming for the purposes of the present exercise, that primary health care covers all the health services from the periphery to the first referral level, i.e., rural health centres plus the cost of identified water supply and sanitation and nutrition programmes. Primary health care constitutes about 54% of the total health sector expenditure. Scrutinizing the medical care expenditure only, the share of primary health care is around 40%. It would be more if expenditure on primary health care aspects of ambulatory care in hospitals, laboratory services, and referral services provided by hospitals could be separated from the aggregated figures. Once again the data would be more meaningful for policy analysis if they were available over a number of years so that trends could be identified. The lack of entry in the self-help column in Table 1A may indicate that methods of estimating the monetary value of donated labour, materials for building and other contributions in kind were not well developed at the time of the case study or simply the difficulty of obtaining such information.

While the government is financing almost 50% of the total health sector (Table 3A), in the case of primary health care its share is only 22.6% and private households have to bear roughly 54% of primary health care costs; foreign aid's share is higher in primary health care than in the financing of the whole sector (19.4% as against 8.4%).

Capital expenditures

Analysis of capital expenditures for the whole sector given in Table 4A shows the following:
— over 94.5% of all capital funds came from external sources; ·
— all government sources financed only about 2.4% of capital expenditure;
— local voluntary bodies are the second largest source of health investment financing with 3% of expenditure.
A further analysis of foreign aid shows the following breakdown:
— 38% district hospitals (including 3% for central hospitals);
— 6.5% health centres and sub-centres;
— 27.3% domestic water supply;

— 27.7% sanitation programmes;

— 0.5% communicable disease control.

Capital expenditure—for example, the construction of health facilities—leads to recurrent costs in the future which will have to be paid by the recipient country. These future costs need to be estimated and included in projections of planned recurrent health expenditure. In the present case, investment in primary health care types of programme is over 57% of total foreign aid.

It is advisable to analyse health investments over several years, in order to avoid the distorting effect in one single year of some construction costs that are spread over a longer period of time.

Broad aspects of data analysis and interpretation

Systematic analysis should compare the available information with national policy objectives and identify further information required for this purpose. For example, how far have the health needs of the population been identified and measured, and by whom? Has the need/demand or part of it been quantified and the cost of meeting it calculated in monetary terms? To what extent is the estimated need met?

It is probable that complete answers to these questions will not be found in any one country. But they may be partly answered by specific studies, such as utilization studies of health facilities (e.g., immunization and maternity and child health programmes), time and motion studies of the use of time by health personnel, household surveys, drug distribution reports, and the views of knowledgeable persons.

The need for information on urban/rural distributions of funds and also on *per caput* expenditure in cities, shanty towns, isolated areas, etc., has also been mentioned. *Per caput* drug expenditure in different population groups is also a useful indicator.

Who is paying for the available health programme? This question can be answered by examining figures on the finance provided in the public sector and by industry, insurance, charity, direct payments by individuals and foreign aid. The geographical distribution of the beneficiaries of each source of finance will show the equity or maldistribution of resources.

Table 1A. Total health sector current expenditures[a]

Area of expenditure	Ministry of health	Other ministries	Local government	Other statutory bodies	Private hospital association (missions)	Industry	Local voluntary bodies (charities)	Direct private payments for health services	Insurance	Self-help/ other private resources	Foreign aid, official	Foreign aid, private	Total
Central hospitals	4 204 000						256 000	86 000					4 546 000
General hospitals	816 000							40 000					856 000
District hospitals	3 437 000				596 000			766 000				463 000	5 262 000
Primary health centres	340 000				87 000			112 000				27 000	566 000
Dispensary/ maternity centres	653 000		43 000	99 000	264 000	42 000		313 000				86 000	1 500 000
Dispensaries	413 000	2 000	29 000	165 000	36 000	545 000		52 000				600	1 242 600
Maternity centres	25 000		300 000										325 000
Mental hospital	240 000												240 000
Services abroad		45 000											45 000
Private practitioners								1 992 000					1 992 000
Traditional healers								588 000					588 000
Drug and dressing supplies	333 000							2 670 000				123 000	3 126 000
Communicable disease controls (i) leprosy	58 000				12 000			38 000				225 000	333 000
(ii) other	296 000	216 000	135 000								367 000	495 000	1 509 000
Domestic water supply		543 000						4 707 000					5 250 000
Sanitation			759 000					232 000					991 000
Nutrition programmes			233 000					2 000			2 000 000		2 235 000
Transport programmes		292 000					119 000						411 000
Headquarters administration	2 324 000		633 000				71 000						3 028 000
Training doctors, dentists											521 000		521 000
Training — other health staff	170 000						49 000				39 000		258 000
Other services		13 000			120 000		233 000	70 000	1 200 000		8 000	178 000	1 822 000
Total	13 309 000	1 111 000 (3.0%)	2 132 000 (5.8%)	264 000 (0.7%)	1 115 000	587 000 (1.6%)	728 000 (2.0%)	11 668 000 (31.8%)	1 200 000 (3.3%)		2 935 000 (8.0%)	1 597 600 (4.4%)	36 646 600 (100%)
Transfers	1 115 000				−1 115 000								
Total	14 424 000 (39.4%)	1 111 000 (3.0%)	2 132 000 (5.8%)	264 000 (0.7%)	120 000	587 000 (1.6%)	728 000 (2.0%)	11 668 000 (31.8%)	1 200 000 (3.3%)		2 935 000 (8.0%)	1 597 600 (4.4%)	36 646 600 (100%)

a This table is a completed version broadly based on the model shown in Table 11 in the manual.

111

Table 2A. Recurrent expenditure for health[a]

Area of expenditure	Million NCU[b]				% share[c]		
	1979	1980	1981	1982	1980	1981	1982
Institutional health care		10 904			29.8		
Ambulatory health services		6 258			17.1		
Special health programmes		4 968			13.5		
Other health-related programmes		8 476			23.1		
Training, management, and other health care services		6 040			16.5		
Total		36 646			100.0		
Primary health care *(as part of total health expenditure)*							
Health centres		566					
Health sub-centres		3 067					
Private practitioners		1 992					
Indigenous healers		588					
Communicable diseases control		1 842					
Drugs, dressings		3 126					
Training of auxiliary personnel		258					
Domestic water supply		5 250					
Sanitation		991					
Nutrition		2 235					
Total		19 915 (54.34%)					

[a] This table is a completed version broadly based on the model shown in Table 1 in the manual.
[b] NCU = national currency unit.
[c] These columns would normally show % change.

Table 3A. Sources of finance for recurrent expenditure for health[a]

Source of finance	Million NCU[b]				% share			
	1979	1980	1981	1982	1979	1980	1981	1982
Total health expenditure								
Government (with missions)		17 931				48.9		
Insurance (private)		1 200				3.3		
Private employers		1 315				3.6		
Private households		11 668				31.8		
Foreign aid (official)		2 935				8.0		
Foreign aid (private)		1 597				4.4		
Total		36 646						
Primary health care								
(as part of total health expenditure)								
Government (with missions)		4 514				22.6		
Insurance (private)		—				—		
Private employers		826				4.2		
Private households		10 706				53.8		
Foreign aid (official)		2 935				14.7		
Foreign aid (private)		934				4.7		
Total		19 915				100.0		

a This table is a completed version broadly based on the model shown in Table 2 in the manual.
b NCU = national currency unit.

113

Table 4A. Total health sector capital expenditures [a]

Area of expenditure	Ministry of health	Other ministries	Local government	Statutory bodies	Private hospital associations (missions)	Local voluntary bodies (charities)	Industry	Direct private payments for health services	Insurance	Self-help/other private resources	Foreign aid, official	Foreign aid, private	Total
Central hospitals	13 000					403 000					34 000		450 000
General hospitals													
District hospitals											3 786 000	1 552 000	5 338 000
Primary health centres												30 000	30 000
Dispensary/maternity centres													
Dispensaries							5 000				87 000	327 000	414 000
Maternity centres						53 000	3 000				322 000	84 000	464 000
Mental hospital											31 000	31 000	31 000
Other institution (specify)													
Services abroad													
Private practicioners													
Traditional healers (specify)													
Drug and dressing supplies													
Communicable disease controls											65 000		65 000
(i) leprosy													
(ii) other													
Domestic water supply										158 000	3 033 000		4 332 000
Sanitation		341 000									3 894 000		3 894 000
Central laboratory service													
Transport													
Headquarters administration													
Training—doctors, dentists													
Training—other health staff													
Other services (specify)													
Transfers													
Total	13 000 (0.1%)	341 000 (2.3%)				456 000 (3.0%)	8 000 (0.1%)			158 000	12 021 000 (80.9%)	2 024 000 (13.6%)	15 021 000 (100%)

[a] This table is a completed version broadly based on the model shown in Table 12 in the manual.

114

Annex 2

ANALYSIS OF COMPLETED TABLES

Most of the questions presented here may be answered by reading completed tables based on the models shown in the manual. The main purpose of listing them is to serve as a reminder. They are modified from teaching material prepared for a training course on financing of health services.[1]

Purpose of expenditure

1. Current account

What is the total expenditure of the health sector:
— in absolute terms?   NC[2] _____
— *per caput*?   NC_____
— % of GNP?   _____
— *per caput* by local administrating
  authority?   Area
                                                        1._____
                                                        2._____
                                                        etc.
— *per caput* in urban areas?   _____
— *per caput* in rural areas?   _____
— % of the total on personal health services?   _____
— *per caput* on personal health
  services?   NC_____
— % of the total on non-personal
  health services?   _____

---

[1] See also reference 8.
[2] NC = national currency.

115

— % of the total expenditure on personal health services on hospital services? _____

— % of the total expenditure on personal health services on health centres, clinics and health posts? _____

— % of the total on health centres, clinics and health posts? _____

— % of the total on primarily preventive services? _____

— % of the total on the national referral hospital(s)? _____

— of the total on general hospitals? _____

— % of the total on indigenous health practitioners? _____

— % of the total on purchases from retail outlets? _____

— % of the total on communicable disease control? _____

— % of the total on domestic water supply? _____

— % of the total on sanitation programmes? _____

— % of the total on nutrition programmes? _____

— % of the total on health education programmes? _____

— % of the total on transport? _____

— % of the total on training other health staff? _____

— on staff in absolute terms? _____

— on doctors employed by government and local authorities?. NC_____

— on drugs, dressings, etc.? NC_____

What is the average cost of:
— a hospital in-patient day (general hospital)? _____
— a hospital in-patient stay (general hospital)? _____
— a case of malaria treated in a general hospital? _____
— a consultation at a clinic with paramedical staff? _____
— a consultation at a health post? _____
— per year on a health centre/clinic with medical staff? _____

116

— per year on a health centre/clinic
with paramedical staff? _____

— per year on a health post with community
health worker only? _____

Ministry of health

What is the ministry of health expenditure:
— as a % of the total government expenditure? _____

What is the:
— % of its expenditure on hospitals? _____
— % of its total on primarily preventive services
expenditure? _____
— % of its total expenditure on hospital
in-patients? _____

Other ministries

What is the:
— % of their total health expenditure on
non-personal health services? _____
— % of their total health expenditure on
primarily preventive services? _____

Local government

What is the:
— % of their total health expenditure on
personal health services? _____
— % of their expenditure on health centres,
clinics and health posts? _____

Missions

What % of their total expenditure is for personal
health service? _____

Industry

What % of expenditure by industry is for
primarily preventive services? _____

What % of expenditure by industry is for
personal health services?
_____

Local voluntary bodies

How much do local voluntary bodies
spend in absolute terms on primarily
preventive services?   NC _____

Direct private payments

Of direct private payments for personal health
services:
— What % is for ambulatory services?   _____
— What % is for indigenous health practitioners? _____
— What % is for services abroad?   _____

Self-help

How much is spent on self-help excluding
donations?   _____

Foreign aid, official

What % of official foreign aid is spent on
primarily preventive services?   _____
If there had been no world food programme
supplies, what would have been the answer to the
last question?   _____

Foreign aid, private

What % of private foreign aid is spent on
primarily preventive services?   _____

Sources of finance

Total

What are the four most important sources of
finance to the health sector, what amount does
each provide, and what % of the total expenditure
does it represent?   _____

	Source	Amount	%
1.	_____	_____	_____
2.	_____	_____	_____
3.	_____	_____	_____
4.	_____	_____	_____
	Total	_____	_____

How much does central and local government
spend on personal health services, and what %
of total expenditure on personal health services
does this represent?   _____

How much does central and local government
spend on non-personal services and what % of
total expenditure on non-personal services does
this represent?   _____

How much do central and local government
sources provide for primarily preventive services
and what % of total expenditure on primarily
preventive services does this represent?   NC _____

General hospital

What % of the expenditure on general hospitals
comes from domestic non-governmental sources? _____

Services abroad

What % of expenditure on services abroad
comes from public sources?   _____

Health centres, clinics and health posts

In which type of clinic or health post is
foreign aid most important, and what %
of total expenditure does it represent for that
service?_____ _____

In what type of clinic or health post are private
payments most important, and what % of the
total expenditure do they represent for that
service?_____ _____

Private practitioners

What proportion of expenditure on private
practitioners is provided by insurance?   _____

Communicable disease control

What is the main source of finance
for communicable disease control,
and what % of the expenditure does it
represent?_____ _____

Domestic water supply

What is the most important source of finance
for domestic water supply,
and what % of the expenditure does it
provide?_____ _____

Sanitation programmes

What % of expenditure on sanitation
programmes comes from the ministry of health? _____

Nutrition programmes

What % of expenditure on nutrition
programmes comes from government sources?   _____

Occupational health services

What % of expenditure on occupational health
services comes from government sources?   _____

Other programmes (Maternal and child health)
How much is spent on the MCH programme,
and what % of this is provided
by government?   NC _____

Transport

What do local authorities spend on transport,
and what % does this represent of total
transport expenditure?   NC _____

Training

If foreign aid for training were cut off, what
would be the % reduction in expenditure on
training:
                              (*a*) doctors   _____
                              (*b*) other staff _____

Transfers

What agency is the main recipient of
transfers, and what is the total amount that it
receives?_____ _____

2. Capital account

What is the total expenditure of the health
sector:
— in absolute terms?   NC _____
— per caput?   NC _____
— % of GNP or GDP?   _____
— % of the total on personal health services?   _____
— % of the total on non-personal health
  services?   _____
— % of the total expenditure on personal health
  services on hospital services?   _____
— % of personal health services on health
  centres, clinics and health posts?   _____
— % of the total on health services, clinics and
  health posts?   _____

— % of the total on primarily preventive
services?

        _____

— % of the total on the national referral
hospital(s)?

        _____

— % of the total on general hospitals? _____

— % of the total on communicable disease
control?

        _____

— % of the total on domestic water supply? _____

— % of the total on sanitation programmes? _____

— % of the total on nutrition programmes? _____

— % of the total on health education
programmes?

        _____

— % of the total on transport? _____

— % of the total on training—other health
staff?

        _____

— % of the total on medical research? _____

What is the average cost of:

— a health centre/clinic with medical staff? _____

— a health centre/clinic with paramedical staff? _____

— a health post with community health worker
only?

        _____

Ministry of health

What is the ministry of health expenditure on
hospitals (including transfers), and the % of its
total expenditure?

        _____

Other ministries

What is the expenditure by other ministries:

— % of their total expenditure on non-personal
health services?

        _____

— % of their total expenditure on primarily
preventive services?

        _____

Local government

What is the expenditure by local government:

— % of their total expenditure on personal
health services?

        _____

— % of their expenditure on personal health services on health centres, clinics and health posts? _____

Industry

What % of expenditure by industry is for primarily preventive services? _____

Local voluntary bodies

What % of the expenditure by local voluntary bodies is for primarily preventive services? _____
How much do local voluntary bodies spend in absolute terms on primarily preventive services? _____

Foreign aid

Comparing the patterns of expenditure of official and private foreign aid, what differences can be identified regarding:

	Official	Private
— the % of the total expenditures on personal health services?	_____	_____
— the % of the total expenditures on personal health services, spent on ambulatory services?	_____	_____
— the % of the total expenditures spent on primarily preventive services?	_____	_____

Sources of finance

Total

What are the two most important sources of finance for the health sector, what amount does each provide and what % of the total expenditure does it represent?

	Source	Amount	%
1.	_____	_____	_____
2.	_____	_____	_____

How much does central and local
government spend on personal health
services, and what % of total expenditure on
personal health services does this represent?   NC _____ % _____
What % of spending on hospitals is provided
by the ministry of health?   _____

Teaching/national referral hospital(s)

What % of the expenditure on the hospital(s) comes from
domestic sources?   _____

General hospitals

What % of the expenditure on these
hospitals comes from foreign aid, and what
% is this of total expenditure on general
hospitals?   NC _____ % _____

Transport

How dependent is the health sector on foreign aid
for the purchase of vehicles?
— % of total current expenditure financed by external
   aid?   _____
— % of total capital expenditure financed by external
   aid?   _____

WHO publications may be obtained, direct or through booksellers, from:

ALGERIA	Société Nationale d'Edition et de Diffusion, 3 bd Zirout Youcef, ALGIERS
ARGENTINA	Carlos Hirsch SRL, Florida 165, Galerías Güemes, Escritorio 453/465, BUENOS AIRES
AUSTRALIA	Hunter Publications, 58A Gipps Street, COLLINGWOOD, VIC 3066 — Australian Government Publishing Service *(Mail order sales)*, P.O. Box 84, CANBERRA A.C.T. 2600; *or over the counter from:* Australian Government Publishing Service Bookshops *at:* 70 Alinga Street, CANBERRA CITY A.C.T. 2600; 294 Adelaide Street, BRISBANE, Queensland 4000; 347 Swanston Street, MELBOURNE, VIC 3000; 309 Pitt Street, SYDNEY, N.S.W. 2000; Mt Newman House, 200 St. George's Terrace, PERTH, WA 6000; Industry House, 12 Pirie Street, ADELAIDE, SA 5000; 156–162 Macquarie Street, HOBART, TAS 7000 — R. Hill & Son Ltd., 608 St. Kilda Road, MELBOURNE, VIC 3004; Lawson House, 10–12 Clark Street, CROW'S NEST, NSW 2065
AUSTRIA	Gerold & Co., Graben 31, 1011 VIENNA I
BANGLADESH	The WHO Programme Coordinator, G.P.O. Box 250, DHAKA 5 — The Association of Voluntary Agencies, P.O. Box 5045, DHAKA 5
BELGIUM	Office international de Librairie, 30 avenue Marnix, 1050 BRUSSELS — *Subscriptions to World Health only:* Jean de Lannoy, 202 avenue du Roi, 1060 BRUSSELS
BRAZIL	Biblioteca Regional de Medicina OMS/OPS, Unidade de Venda de Publicações, Caixa Postal 20.381, Vila Clementino, 04023 SÃO PAULO, S.P.
BURMA	*see* India, WHO Regional Office
CANADA	Canadian Public Health Association, 1335 Carling Avenue, Suite 210, OTTAWA, Ont. K1Z 8N8. *Subscription orders, accompanied by cheque made out to the* Royal Bank of Canada, Ottawa, Account World Health Organization, *may also be sent to the* World Health Organization, P.O. Box 1800, Postal Station B, OTTAWA, Ont. K1P 5R5
CHINA	China National Publications Import & Export Corporation, P.O. Box 88, BEIJING (PEKING)
CYPRUS	"MAM", P.O. Box 1722, NICOSIA
CZECHO-SLOVAKIA	Artia, Ve Smeckach 30, 111 27 PRAGUE 1
DENMARK	Munksgaard Export and Subscription Service, Nørre Søgade 35, 1370 COPENHAGEN K (Tel: +45 1 12 85 70)
ECUADOR	Librería Científica S.A., P.O. Box 362, Luque 223, GUAYAQUIL
EGYPT	Osiris Office for Books and Reviews, 50 Kasr El Nil Street, CAIRO
FIJI	The WHO Programme Coordinator, P.O. Box 113, SUVA
FINLAND	Akateeminen Kirjakauppa, Keskuskatu 2, 00101 HELSINKI 10
FRANCE	Librairie Arnette, 2 rue Casimir-Delavigne, 75006 PARIS
GERMAN DEMOCRATIC REPUBLIC	Buchhaus Leipzig, Postfach 140, 701 LEIPZIG
GERMANY, FEDERAL REPUBLIC OF	Govi-Verlag GmbH, Ginnheimerstrasse 20, Postfach 5360, 6236 ESCHBORN — W. E. Saarbach, Postfach 101 610, Follerstrasse 2, 5000 COLOGNE 1 — Alex. Horn, Spiegelgasse 9, Postfach 3340, 6200 WIESBADEN
GHANA	Fides Enterprises, P.O. Box 1628, ACCRA
GREECE	G.C. Eleftheroudakis S.A., Librairie internationale, rue Nikis 4, ATHENS (T. 126)
HAITI	Max Bouchereau, Librairie "A la Caravelle", Boîte postale 111-B, PORT-AU-PRINCE
HONG KONG	Hong Kong Government Information Services, Beaconsfield House, 6th Floor, Queen's Road, Central, VICTORIA
HUNGARY	Kultura, P.O.B. 149, BUDAPEST 62 — Akadémiai Könyvesbolt, Váci utca 22, BUDAPEST V
ICELAND	Snaebjørn Jonsson & Co., P.O. Box 1131, Hafnarstraeti 9, REYKJAVIK
INDIA	WHO Regional Office for South-East Asia, World Health House, Indraprastha Estate, Mahatma Gandhi Road, NEW DELHI 110002 — Oxford Book & Stationery Co., Scindia House, NEW DELHI 110001; 17 Park Street, CALCUTTA 700016 (*Sub-agent*)
INDONESIA	P. T. Kalman Media Pusaka, Pusat Perdagangan Senen, Block 1, 4th Floor, P.O. Box 3433/Jkt, JAKARTA
IRAQ	Ministry of Information, National House for Publishing, Distributing and Advertising, BAGHDAD
IRELAND	TDC Publishers, 12 North Frederick Street, DUBLIN 1
ISRAEL	Heiliger & Co., 3 Nathan Strauss Street, JERUSALEM 94227
ITALY	Edizioni Minerva Medica, Corso Bramante 83–85, 10126 TURIN; Via Lamarmora 3, 20100 MILAN
JAPAN	Maruzen Co. Ltd., P.O. Box 5050, TOKYO International, 100–31
KUWAIT	The Kuwait Bookshops Co. Ltd., Thunayan Al-Ghanem Bldg, P.O. Box 2942, KUWAIT
LAO PEOPLE'S DEMOCRATIC REPUBLIC	The WHO Programme Coordinator, P.O. Box 343, VIENTIANE
LEBANON	The Levant Distributors Co. S.A.R.L., Box 1181, Makdassi Street, Hanna Bldg, BEIRUT
LUXEMBOURG	Librairie du Centre, 49 bd Royal, LUXEMBOURG
MALAWI	Malawi Book Service, P.O. Box 30044, Chichiti, BLANTYRE 3